BEATING TIME

by the same author

The Left in Britain 1956–68

Health in Danger, the crisis in the NHS

(with An Deker)
The Book of the Year

(with Phil Evans)
The Joke Works

(with Syd Shelton and Red Saunders)
Day In The Life of London

BEATING TIME
DAVID WIDGERY

DESIGN: **RUTH GREGORY**
ANDY DARK

(A TIGERSTRIPE BOOK)

Chatto & Windus
London

Published in 1986 by
Chatto & Windus
40 William IV Street
London WC2N 4DF

ISBN 0 7011 2985 9

Photoset by Rowland Phototypesetting Ltd
Bury St Edmunds, Suffolk
Printed in Great Britain by
Butler & Tanner Ltd, Frome, Somerset

Adrian Mitchell's poem *'Sorry bout that'* from
Collected Poems 1953–79 is quoted by kind
permission of Alison & Busby.

To Annie, **Jesse** and **Juliet**

We should stop trying to teach, and begin to learn again; from Africa and Asia as much as Russia or America. We should begin to like ourselves, and less our grandfathers. We should banish anyone who says *Don't* (whatever his authority and even if he is right) and hearken to anyone who says *Do*, however crazy. We should be gay, libertarian, serious and energetic, intoxicated with life, not stopping all the time to pick its nose. We should mock smug naysayers, applaud the adventurous. We should stop being *English*, and become English men and women.

Colin MacInnes
in Sterilities (and Virilities)
(Encounter, 1963)

C O N T E N T S

INTRODUCTION   8

CHAPTER 1: **THE DEATH OF ALTAB ALI**   11

CHAPTER 2: **BRICK LANE BLUES**   19

CHAPTER 3: **WHAT'S GOING ON?**   35

CHAPTER 4: **ROCKIN' AGAINST IT**   53

BREWING IT UP   75

CHAPTER 5: **THE REAL GANGSTERS COME**   79

CHAPTER 6: **GOTTA KEEP ON KEEPING ON**   111

TIME CHECK   124

HEROES AND VILLAINS   125

NAME CHECK   126

INDEX   127

INTRODUCTION

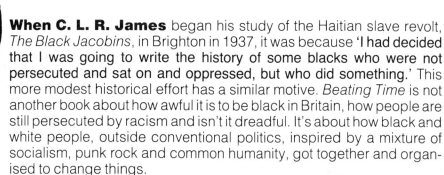

When C. L. R. James began his study of the Haitian slave revolt, *The Black Jacobins*, in Brighton in 1937, it was because 'I had decided that I was going to write the history of some blacks who were not persecuted and sat on and oppressed, but who did something.' This more modest historical effort has a similar motive. *Beating Time* is not another book about how awful it is to be black in Britain, how people are still persecuted by racism and isn't it dreadful. It's about how black and white people, outside conventional politics, inspired by a mixture of socialism, punk rock and common humanity, got together and organised to change things.

It was temporary. We didn't stop racial attacks, far less racism. Indeed the gloomy political predictions made by Rock Against Racism about the social consequences of Mrs Thatcher's self-serving political philosophy, Britain's deeply embedded involvement with the regime in South Africa and the remorseless militarisation of our police force, dismissed at the time as infantile hyperbole, have proved only too accurate. But the simple, electrifying idea that pop music can be about more than entertainment has endured and deepened. Band Aid, Live Aid and Artists Against Apartheid have sent rock writers back to Woodstock and the hippies in search of precedents. But it was Rock Against Racism (RAR) and the more militant traditions within music and politics with which we identified that first set music and politics dancing with each other. And we did it without financial aid from commissions for equality or local authorities and with very little encouragement from the media who adore campaigns against hunger in Africa but are a lot less interested in identifying and confronting racism in their own back yard. RAR was what we said it was: a rank-and-file movement of the ordinary, the unknown and the unkempt. Which is why it worked.

'Nothing's really changed. They're doing exactly the same things, selling arms to South Africa, killing blacks on the streets, people are living in poverty, it's the same.'
John Lennon

I heard Paul Holborow, the National Secretary of the Anti-Nazi League, at a meeting of the Socialist Workers Party recently. Alongside him were teachers from the Daneford School in Bethnal Green, East London, taking action against attacks on their Asian pupils, someone from Broadwater Farm estate describing the police's painstaking revenge on the black tenants there and a campaigner from Waltham Forest documenting the terrifying sequence of racial arson attacks in outer East London. The struggle goes on, across distinctly more difficult terrain than in the late 1970s. RAR and the ANL seemed a long time ago. But the speakers again and again referred to those campaigns as the proof that things can be done, not just endured. And to something else, a glimpse of a different sort of society, a moment of inspiration which will last a lifetime. For a while we managed to create, in our noisy, messy, unconventional way, an emotional alternative to nationalism and patriotism, a celebration of a different kind of pride and solidarity. You don't beat time easily, it takes as much preparation, skill and attention to detail as a successful bullion robbery. But those moments are the only ones worth stealing.

David Widgery, Hackney, December 1985

'My brain was like a crazy TV
set flicking picture stories in
colour black-and-white.'
Charlie Mingus

THE DEATH OF ALTAB ALI

The park in Whitechapel where Altab Ali was killed is not much more than a field with some trees. A scattering of headstones and a mausoleum dated 1774 reveal it was once a churchyard, perhaps secularised by one of those improving organisations of Victorian liberalism like Lord Meath's Metropolitan Public Gardens Committee. Nowadays St Mary's churchyard is one of several East End *itchy parks* which provide informal accommodation for vagrant men and women who would at least have been housed indoors in the nineteenth century. In spring, its principal inhabitants are tramps, some quite young, who sit together quarrelling amiably, passing cider bottles fortified with meths and investigating the layers of their ragged clothes. Sometimes there is a flurry as a drinker claws in the direction of a passer-by, attempts to embrace the sky or exultantly hoists a glittering can of Special Brew into the sunlight. Weekend lovers occasionally use its benches to cuddle and spread their Sunday supplements after a tour of the Whitechapel Gallery. At lunchtime Bloom's salt-beef sandwiches – the fast food of the Diaspora – are munched inside the park. Otherwise few would use the park except as a short cut from Brick Lane through to the Commercial Road, past the disused flats, ugly unlet office blocks and the gantrylike crucifix above St Boniface's Church. **'Did you know that "Admiral" Parker, the leader of the mutiny of Spithead and the Nore in 1797, was buried here?'** a docker friend proudly told me. **'After they cut his bloody head off.'** Now St Mary's will be remembered for another death.

It was still quite light on 4th May 1978 when the 25-year-old clothing machinist Altab Ali made his way from the small factory just off Brick Lane where he had been at work since early morning. His home was a room in Wapping. He left his workmates, bought some food for his evening meal and then crossed Whitechapel High Street intending to cut through the park and into Commercial Road by the Furniture College.

It was still light when his attackers set about him, lunging at his throat and chest with a knife until the major vessels of his thorax were severed. Still light as they ran away leaving him humped up in the gutter, gasping for breath, howling with pain, not just bleeding but spurting blood from his chest. For perhaps a quarter of an hour he lay there, exsanguinating, making the

'The crux of the matter was that we had refused to act as refugees; as helpless, well-behaved children. For that last possession, our humanity, we were willing to fight.'

Mahmoud Mamdani

Altab Ali's funeral march, Whitechapel, 14th May 1978.

desperate, frothy cough characteristic of this type of wound.

At the London Hospital receiving room, only a few hundred yards away, 'doctors fought for his life', or so the papers said. I have spent enough time in casualty departments to imagine the scene. The fishing with arterial clamps to shut off the bleeding vessels, the drip sets threaded into collapsed veins to replace the spilt blood, the rushing in and out with cross-match forms. In the middle of all the activity, someone is slowly, hopelessly dying.

Who was the man on the operating table? Who was Altab Ali? He was one of the invisible, one of the people who do not matter. A Bengali from Wapping. One of the people who are supposed to be grateful for even being allowed to enter our great civilisation. Mr Hossein, his brother, says, '**He was a hard-working man who was very fond of his family. He got on very well with everyone.**' Mr Safra saw him quite often in the café. '**Oh, Mr Ali. Very nice man. Very quiet. No trouble, no trouble.**' Alok Biswas is getting tired of the question. '**Who *was* Altab Ali?**' I ask unwisely. He shouts back at me from the doorway: '**He was a man who worked for his living, that's who. He was a man who bought meat to eat with his friends. He was like any one of us.**'

The next time we meet, Alok apologises for shouting. But I know what made him angry. Alive Altab Ali was ordinary, so no one cared or noticed. He was a man who had to be killed to become a subject of interest to white society.

The death of Altab Ali threw into stark relief the general level of racial violence in the East End, the indifference of the police and the prejudices of the non-Asians. Youth at the funeral raised placards: *No more racial killings, Self-defence, no offence* and *No police cover-up*. Over each slogan they had put the silk-screened outline of a man lying in the gutter with blood coming from his eye and chest, his hands imploring to the sky.

For socialists, random violence by working-class people against a fellow worker of another skin colour was devastating. Roger Huddle, an ex-mod typographer who had joined the Socialist Workers Party from the Young Socialists in the early 1960s, still remembers it as

> 'England's place — what is England's place? To carry civilisation through the world? . . . in these days, I begin to wonder if civilisation itself is, may not be sometimes so much adulterated as scarcely to be worth the carrying anyhow it cannot be worth much, when it is necessary to kill a man in order to make him accept it.'
> **William Morris**

a frightening period. It came up like a time bomb. You'd just come out of 1972–74 when the workers had brought down a Tory government. And the Labour Party was in power. And you were waiting for the honeymoon to be over and the upturn of the workers' struggles to start again. And suddenly there were people strutting the streets of Walthamstow with swastikas.

Dan Jones, who was both secretary of the Tower Hamlets Trades Council and a youth worker in Spitalfields, remembers '**us all saying to ourselves, is this what white working-class Londoners are really like?**'

For me it took the blood of Altab Ali to mark the downturn. I was twenty-one in 1968 when the student Left took on the world and seemed, for a while, to be outwitting the bureaucrats and the war lords of the Pentagon and the Kremlin. Student romanticism matured and merged into the rejuvenated socialism of the rank-and-file movement which powered the great strike waves of the seventies and, in 1974, overturned a government. But now, in 1978, instead of exuberant advance, the film had gone into reverse. A nerveless, unconvincingly avuncular Labour government, facing the first major international depression since the thirties, had grovelled to the IMF, pioneered the public-sector cuts and turned on its own traditional supporters. For the first

Altab Ali Defence Committee placard.

Dan Jones

BLOOD ON THE STREETS

time in my generation's political experience, the Left was on the defensive and the extreme Right was on the streets.

Altab Ali's killing took place on the night of the 1978 local council elections where, in Tower Hamlets, the National Front were challenging Labour in forty-three of the fifty possible seats, instead of their usual eight or nine. Even though they polled poorly, the number of NF candidates and the over-amplified noise of fascist loudspeaker vans gave an atmosphere heavy with the static of racial antagonism. And that atmosphere had undoubtedly been heightened by an important speech earlier in the year by Margaret Hilda Thatcher. In her dainty way, Mrs Thatcher had firmly linked the fears of

'Racism is moral in a racist society.'

Remi Kapo

Brewery workers ambushed leaving work, Three Mill Lane, Bow, 6th July 1978.

Unknown

post-imperial Britain with prejudice against black immigrants. In January 1978 she said, on Granada TV,

> **I think people** are really rather afraid that this country might be rather swamped by people with a different culture and, you know, the British character has done so much for democracy and law, and has done so much throughout the world, that if there is any fear that it might be swamped, people are going to be really rather hostile to those coming in.

Mrs Thatcher's comments were boil-in-the-bag xenophobia. She reheated a very old recipe, saying, in effect: yes, take your fears as reality and act on them; yes, it's only British to be hostile to foreigners; no, they are not civilised like us. Single-handedly, she had recuperated overt racism into the Parliamentary tradition. For it's the very sanctimoniousness of those words and the pained poshness of the voice that uttered them which fuels and authenticates the street savagery. It's the nod from the C O to the privates that they can put the boot in. Alok Biswas commented:

'I'm not trying to be a pretend teenager, or even a pretend mid-twenties person, but just somebody who was born in the '50s, grew up with those values, saw them crash and also what my generation has become. There *is* a way of keeping your self respect . . .'
Tom Robinson

> **The police are** falling over each other suddenly to find out who is the agent of Altab Ali's death. I have no idea. But of who is responsible I am clear in my mind. That's Mrs Thatcher. She talks of us as aliens. She says we must be kept out and made to leave – says that everywhere we are a problem people. So it's just no good for her to throw up her hands in horror when some crazy kids, wound up by her, do this murder.

What we were witnessing in the mean streets of the East End was the revival of a murderous racism we thought had been decisively defeated four decades ago. There was no motive for the killing other than skin hatred. The assailants didn't look for Altab Ali's wages or even bother to take his dinner. They didn't know him well enough to hold a grudge against him. Yet they cut his throat in a chilling mixture of the offhand and the deadly. If this kind of murder were to be accepted, if it was quietly tidied away while the police got on with their inquiries, it would have implied that the Asians of East London were somehow less human, less entitled to live than the rest of us, not even allowed the luxury of being left alone. '**And that**,' my docker friend Micky Fenn, then a senior shop steward in the Royal Group, lectured me as we passed the Special Branch men with their beer guts outside Aldgate East tube station on our way to Altab Ali's funeral,

British Movement skins, Goulston Street, Aldgate.

Syd Shelton

> **that is just** the end. I mean, it's different to label someone because they are a Tory. Because they can help that, they can think about that. But to label someone because they were born with a certain colour skin, I find that absolutely repugnant. There's no hope, no way out of it. Because someone's got no control over how they were born. And that's what was so disturbing about these kids, you know, these skins out in Barking and Becontree and Dagenham way when you talk to them. Half of them have families from Ireland anyway. They've got some ideas about what's

British citizens, legally settled, protesting their innocence after a police 'passport raid' at 3 am, Spitalfields, 1978.

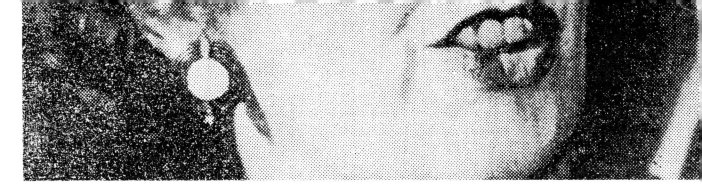

'Truly, I live in dark times!
The guileless word is folly. A
    smooth forehead
Suggests insensitivity. The
    man who laughs
Has simply not yet had
The terrible news.'
    Bertolt Brecht

Chris Davis (Network)

wrong with the world. But their only way of explaining anything is the easy one . . . black. Because they can see them.

We – meaning everybody whose responses were still intact – had not only to stop the murders and try to understand how our imperial past was giving racial overtones to present-day frustrations. It was essential to get to those young people before the real gangsters did.

Ten days later, 7000 people are milling about in the park where Altab Ali died. To march from there to Hyde Park; to mourn, but in a spirit of resistance. In such sluicing rain that banners disintegrate, newspapers are sodden and shoes leak. The older Asians, being British of the old school, have brought macs and neatly rolled umbrellas. People make hats out of their placards, some of the Asian youths have transparent rain caps embossed with flowers and two have joke bowlers with *I'm backing Britain* Union Jack hat bands. There are no Asian women to be seen. People take snapshots of each other. It is an occasion, a serious one. The familiar faces who hold together anti-fascist activity in East London are there. The Asian contingents, organised from all over Britain in a matter of days, are sombre and determined.

Elders with astrakhan hats and white goatees sport anti-racist lapel badges, white socialists are trusted members of the stewarding team. The youth wheel and chant in the centre of the soaking park. The first sound is the traditional Islamic call to the faithful: 'Allah wakhbar', God will conquer. Then there is a faster fiercer chant, of anger, of vengeance, of revolt. An enormous rattle of thunder splits the rain.

Askan is one of the youths who organised the march. He is part of the emerging emergency leadership of a new generation of London Bengalis. His grin is almost permanent and has that air of cockiness common to East London kids whatever their skin colour. He struggles to put his feelings in proper, diplomatic order. 'These racial attacks, they are getting worse all the time. Worse since the National Front on the scene. Worse since Mrs Thatcher's speech. We're not getting co-operation from the police. Mr Callaghan and his colleagues, do they realise what is happening all the time to our people? And Mrs Thatcher.' He pauses, groping for a suitable, judicious phrase. His mate in a plastic rally jacket and cap gives a sudden, piercing look, then spits one word to the ground: 'Thatcher-Shit.' Askan is fifteen.

My old patient, Mr Safra from the café, who is partially blind, has found his way to the demonstration. 'Murder, murder, murder; it's getting bloody ridiculous. How about us having a bit of law and order for a change?' He has lived in Whitechapel for nearly fifteen years but never had cause to go to Hyde Park before.

Altab Ali's killers were teenage boys: Roy Arnold, aged seventeen, of Limehouse, Carl Ludlow, aged seventeen, of Bow, and an unnamed mixed-race boy from Poplar, aged sixteen. It was the sixteen-year-old who did the stabbing and when the police asked him why, his chilling reply was 'For no reason at all.' He stated, as if it were commonplace, 'If we saw a Paki we used to have a go at them. We would ask for money and beat them up. I've beaten up Pakis on at least five occasions.' To these boys, simply by being Asian Altab Ali was a potential target. For one, the killing of another black was a kind of initiation ceremony, his ticket of admission into white male society. Paki-bashing was for these boys as much part of the ritual of growing up as the first puff on the filter tip. And it started about as early.

But after the march, no permanent commemoration of Altab Ali was left in St Mary's churchyard. No public subscription has been raised to place a

'Should any future Conservative, Powellite or National Front government succeed in repatriating immigrants, we will hope to return your emigrants to take up the vacancies. This would mean that for every West Indian or Indian deported, we could send you, on a fair statistical basis, as replacements, one 'pakeha' New Zealander, four Canadians, half a South African white, part of a white Rhodesian, and no fewer than 50 American WASPS. It would take some time for you to absorb the extra 200 million people involved, but there is no reason why, if phased over a decent period and with sensible birth control measures being taken, England should not be the exclusive home of those who speak English and live in the English manner.'
Ngata Te Korou

Unknown

Dan Jones

memorial where he lay. There were no condolences from No. 10 or apologies from the Mayor of Tower Hamlets dissociating the citizens of the borough from the killing. Backbenchers did not rend Westminster with adjectival outbursts against the men of violence at large in Whitechapel.

In the five years between 1976 and 1981, calculated the historian Peter Fryer, thirty-one black people in Britain were murdered by racists. It's not, well, nice to think too hard about David Oluwale, kicked to death by Leeds policemen for a bit of sport, or Gurdip Singh Chaggar taunted and then stabbed to death by a gang of drunks in Southall, or Ishaque Ali strangled outside the Electricity Board office in Lower Clapton Road, or Shamir Kassam, herself eight months pregnant and her three sons finally burnt to death in their home in Chadwell Heath in 1985 after two earlier arson attacks.

The truth is that there are few more important murders to solve in modern Britain. We have to follow such crimes to the recesses of the psyche where spoilt ambition and acrid jealousies jostle with political desperation and imperial fantasy. We need to examine the social conditions in which these murders arise with the attention to detail a forensic pathologist applies to his clues. Just as the pathologist is able to draw from tiny quantities of diseased tissue conclusions about the sick body's overall state, so by investigating the individual racial murder we can draw more general conclusions about the indifference, ignorance and moral cowardice in which they flourish. For what matters as much as the fact of Ali's murder is that it was somehow not considered real (because Asians are not considered 'real' people), police investigation was within a routine low-key framework (since 'racial attack' was not in 1978 a category which existed) and the general reaction was to pretend that the problem right under our noses had not even happened.

This grim echo of imperialism was not animated by conquest or buttressed by religious belief. It was revenge against nothing less than history itself. 'The doctrine of white supremacy begins in Europe and now it has crossed over that water and come back to Europe,' says James Baldwin. 'It is having the same effect in all European cities as it had in all the American cities I grew up in. What's happening in London, Amsterdam, Berlin and Paris is what was happening in America when I was a little boy. The doctrine's come home to roost and no one knows what happens now.'

It was high Victorian Britain, not Nazi Germany, that sharpened and systematised the idea of white supremacy and Europe enforced it upon the world. In its name empires were erected, civilisations destroyed, cultures eradicated and hundreds of thousands killed. It was the unspoken maxim that wrote our history books, erected our monuments and saluted our flags and

Socialist Worker
PAPER OF THE SOCIALIST WORKERS PARTY 10p

INSIDE
SITTING ON TIM
Will the Spania
Britain? —back
GRUNWICKS
An obituary—p
HUMAN BLOOD
—page fill

BIRTH OF OU POWER

8000 strike against raci

Solidarity strike called by the Hackney and Tower Hamlets Defence Committee, 17th July 1978.

E stands for Empire, built upon blood;

I stands for India, never yet quelled;

J is for Jail, where good rebels are held.

Above: **From a workers' alphabet.** Below: **Sabu, star of _Elephant Boy_.**

India; Highlanders stand to attention as the Last Post is played at sunset.

our monarchs. High imperialism was able to treat its conquered colonies as virtual plantations, wrenching the native economy into line with British needs, buying off reliable princes and obedient chiefs and carefully clothing the robbery in the quaint rigmarole of colonial government. The system was saturated by racism. **'One meets these "nigger-haters" everywhere,'** writes the liberal imperialist Lieutenant-Colonel Osburn, as late as 1930 in _Must England Lose India?_,

from Shanghai to Delhi: from Rangoon to the Service Clubs in Pall Mall. They are usually quite intelligent and even influential men, but imbued with the point of view which Mr Kipling so eloquently voiced. They believe themselves to be a kind of Anglican Almighty who as far as _natives_ are concerned, _can do no wrong_. Quite genially over a whisky and soda the returned Indian officer, Indian official, or business man, will describe the Hindus as _stinking niggers_, _seditious swine_, or, by some other happily chosen obscene equivalent in Hindustani.

Even their sadism was refined: in the suppression of the national rising known to Europeans as _the Indian mutiny_, which broke out in 1857 and in which Altab Ali's ancestors could have fought, the British army's revenge included the burning of villages and their occupants, the blowing of men from cannon mouths, and mass hangings. But this was supposed to be over. In the twentieth century, the trade mission had replaced the Governor's residence, the nationalist leaders became the local ruling class ('transfer of stewardship' as it was known in grouse-moorese), the multinational superfirms kept a monopoly on research, technology, finance and thus international politics. And, by and large, the whites tried to stop hitting the blacks (and got other blacks to hit the blacks for them). Now when the CIA and other international agencies of its type install and dethrone successive leaders, as in Bangladesh, they take great care to manipulate the situation at some distance.

However, although members of the British ruling class are trained to discard the belief system they once utilised if it should clash with the present needs of their class, the lower orders aren't so amnesiac. They have more to forget and less to be cynical about. As a new depression accelerated post-imperial Britain's decline, it seemed as if the ghosts of 1857 were unleashed again, no longer pukka, pith-helmeted and fortified with whisky and Indian tonic water, but street killers in wet plimsolls, stalking the descendants of the colonised in the back streets of imperialism's oldest capital.

BRICK LANE BLUES

London is one of the oldest ports in maritime history and its docklands are an encyclopaedia of national origins. Besides the Angles, Saxons, Jutes, Scots, Vikings, Danes and their children, there were the nonconforming Huguenots who fled France after the Revocation of the Edict of Nantes in 1685 and who have left us their rooftop workshops and their fine bow-window fronts. Then there are the Irish, starved from their native land to labour in London, who constructed those three remarkable Hawksmoor churches, Christ Church Spitalfields, St George's in the East and St Anne's, Limehouse, as well as the intricate indentations of the docks. The refugees from the terrible pogroms of 1882 which followed the anti-Semitic Tsarist ukase in Russia and Poland were saved, in Whitechapel, from the worst Jewish martyrdom until the Holocaust itself.

It was these East European survivors who created the classic Jewish ghetto of which Brick Lane was the High Street. A sizeable Chinese community was established in Limehouse as early as 1880. Then, after the First World War, seamen from Somalia, Ethiopia and East Africa settled in the old Cable Street area, joined by Mediterranean peoples from North Italy, Greece, Cyprus and Malta. After the Second World War came communities of Sikhs and West Indians, including clusters from the smaller Francophone islands, and more Irish Catholic settlers. In the fifties, Scots, Liverpudlians and Geordie construction workers came for work and stayed and married. And most recently have come the Bengalis from the Sylhet district of northeast Bangladesh.

'What I am trying to say is that what blacks have been doing in Britain over the last 25 years is making history.'
Linton Kwesi Johnson

The Brune Street soup kitchen, Whitechapel.

So as well as the Smiths and the Browns and the Greens there are the Jacobs and Cohens and Zackorys, the O'Reillys and Branagans and Conollys, the Matadeens and Micaleffs, and the Singhs and Rahmans and Begums.

The East End is an area acclimatised to successive waves of migration; a permanent point of entry and a place of constant departures. It is therefore a mixture of the international and the insular. One of the cradles of the Labour movement, it is also the birthplace of British fascism: the first meeting of the British Brothers League was held in Stepney in May 1901. Organised by Major Eden Evans Gordon, an imperialist and former Indian Army officer who was MP for Stepney, the League's mass meetings began with patriotic street

Below: **The Cheshire Street synagogue, Whitechapel.** Bottom: **East London tailor's workshop before 1914.**

Dan Jones

> 'If Britishness consists of going round the world sneering at foreigners then I don't want to know.'
> **Robert Wyatt**

processions and the playing on the organ of *Soldier Of The Queen* and *Home Sweet Home*. But these rallies ended with inflammatory speeches against the 'so-called refugees' only in London 'because they wanted our money', the brutal removal of objectors and the chanting of 'Wipe them out'. In 1898, one third of Stepney Council were publicans elected on an anti-Jew, pro-booze ticket. But East London was also the home of international socialists who upheld the right of asylum, warned against the xenophobia which would arise from workers 'trying to think imperially' and argued, in an East End socialist weekly newspaper of 1903, that 'to His Majesty's Government, the alien question is a matter of locality – and money. If you are a millionaire you are welcome in Park Lane, but if you are a Jewish tailor flying from injustice and persecution, you are not welcome in England at all.'

The same arguments and politics continue in new idioms and are compounded by the social problems of the modern city. The sociologists tell us that the inner city is a sink into which have sunk the least able of the urban working class. The net effects of post-war housing, transport, education and employment policies have led the successful skilled working class to move outwards in a series of concentric rings, creating the proletarian suburbia of Essex. Those who have got on, have got out. And they have abandoned their memories and their elderly relatives to the geriatric hospitals and the social workers. Those left behind are the old and the unskilled; no longer wanted on what's left of the job market. And they have been joined by the post-war black and brown migration, sometimes itself in transit to another location. More and more of this population is Giro-dependent – the pensioners of an ungenerous state. But they have different ages, different ethnic origins and different needs, none of which are properly satisfied in the drab, uniform, inconvenient amenities which house them.

So the borough contains both people passing through and long-standing residents now concerned with establishing a family or enjoying a well-earned retirement, and a much more complicated and sophisticated proletariat than the statistics of deprivation, grim as they certainly are, might suggest. The dull tower blocks conceal a cosmopolitan population which has weaved a way of life with its own complicated communications systems, pecking orders and intricate politenesses.

So there are no stereotypes. Just Jewish anti-Semites and Jamaican High Tories and Irish royalists and depressive barrow boys and gay taxi drivers and Anglo-Saxon spivs and Welsh Manicheans and African mannequins and Sri Lankan policewomen and Sikh break dancers. And a whole lot of people who think of themselves as *'old East Enders'* have a little moan about *'the coloureds'* but would complain if the colour and variety and clamour vanished from the markets and cafés and nurseries and shops and hospitals, pubs and schools, so that the place became as grey as Southend out of season. Or if the coloured nurse and the family in the paper shop and the black scout-troop leader or the team that won the disco-dancing trophy suddenly disappeared. As the happily married gay taxi driver from Bow once told me in the York Hall steam rooms: 'We can make a cockney out of anyone with a bit of class.'

Skin colour is only one, probably not especially important, determiner of social acceptability. The souring frustrations and unscrupulous energy of the inner city are held in common. People who will state emphatically that they are 'against immigration' often have West Indian friends, don't dislike black people at all and object very strongly to the National Front. But the truth is also that people in the white community who are mates with Afro-Caribbean cockneys still find it hard to cope with Asian neighbours (and probably vice versa). So in the mid-seventies it was impossible to predict whether East Enders would react to the clashes which were to centre on Brick Lane with the scapegoat nationalism and anti-alien prejudice always just below the surface of the Tory working man and woman or with the more cosmopolitan and radical outlook of East End socialism.

The importance of Brick Lane is that it has all these contradictions, culture clashes and political history compressed into a single street. It is inevitably seen as the home of Asian culture and religion in modern East London, although this view is overplayed now and rightly resented by the large non-Spitalfields Asian communities that are getting themselves organised in St Katherine's, Shadwell, St Mary's and Bromley by Bow. But it displays clear and heartening evidence of the preceding Huguenot and Jewish mass migration and assimilation into East London in the sixteenth and nineteenth centuries.

Dan Jones

Christ Church Spitalfields by Nicholas Hawksmoor, looming over the vegetable market.

Nina Saunders

A clothing shop in Brick Lane.

Nina Saunders

The Lane itself runs from Bethnal Green to Whitechapel, starting at a modern council estate full of shouting kids with BMXs and footballs, and ending three-quarters of a mile further south alongside the Art Deco façade of the Whitechapel Art Gallery. Walking down it, you pass a brewery, a mosque, a brothel, an ultramodern health centre, numerous restaurants, food shops, sari centres and surplus stores, a cinema and several shipping agents, the rooms where the first ever Jewish Socialist Manifesto was drawn up and the place where Jack the Ripper's last victim was found in 1888. It's a long, thin streak of a street which often has an edgy air, as if something has just happened.

In Jack the Ripper's day, the south part of the Lane was a hotbed of villainy, fisticuffs and prostitution, a Victorian red-light district famous for its music halls, gin palaces and fights. The area around Flower and Dean Street, then known as Flowery Dean Street, consisted of cheap lodging houses, thieves' kitchens and *'doubles'* – furnished rooms where *'the brides'* used to take their sexual customers. To this day prostitutes still pay a terrible toll in violent attacks and murders. In Victorian Spitalfields the rent collectors and police were kept at bay for months on end by the most organised and disorderly tenements. In those days the police hardly dared enter the area and the succeeding generations of residents have remained suspicious, with some justice, of the law.

It's *Brick* Lane because brick making was its first industry. Like many of the *noxious* trades, the brick makers had been cast out from within the city walls. The brewery which sits halfway down the street was established by Joseph Truman four centuries ago. It remained a family business until 1971 and still functions today, with the old brewhouse repeatedly modified and modernised to deal with cold storage, bottling and metal kegs, and the staff, who included draymen, copper smiths and coopers as well as brewers, often giving traditionally loyal service. It remains the exception to Brick Lane work places in that it is industrial and organised: the ACTSS 1/17 Branch produced a good *alternative plan* for the brewery in 1983.

The garment trade remains based in small workshops and the home. High Street chains like C & A and Debenhams do not build factories but make their profits through extensive sub-subcontracting which ends up in self-exploiting workshops where machinists work piece rate and have no defence against long lay-offs when business is slack. This isolation is not insuperable, as the Leeds clothing workers proved in 1970 when strikers from the bigger work-shops marched round the back streets pulling workers in the sweatshops out on strike too. But in East London, successive waves of migration into this subeconomy have further complicated the picture, both hindering trade union organisation (by often inadvertent undercutting of wage rates) and providing new cultural roots and routes for the traditions of labour organisa-tion. Nationally Asian rank-and-file trade unionists, of both sexes, have been crucial to the modern British labour movement and the strikes they have led, from Woolfs Rubber Southall via Grunwick, Mansfield Hosiery, Chix and Injection Mouldings, read like an industrial roll of honour. But in East London it is a process which is taking time and ingenuity. After all, it took from the first great strike by immigrant Jewish clothing workers for the twelve-hour day in 1889 through to the 1912 strike by the West End tailors of the next generation to establish the first successful tailoring unions. And the Bangladeshi trade unionists face the same old problems of race prejudice, language and exploitation by family and by co-religionists as well as the new ones of multinational manufacture and anti-union legislation.

So the heavy sweetness of hops and the whirr of sewing machines from upper rooms are still the most characteristic smell and sound of the Lane's intimate mix of manufacture, dwelling and leisure. The street was already built up by the mid-eighteenth century when much of Tower Hamlets was still farm land and recreation grounds. Its pattern remains today. The brewery has been rebuilt with a mirror-window façade which hides the chimneys and reflects an elegant Georgian row and the considerable monies made out of the working man's pint over the centuries even if now it's brewing up fake Budweiser and ersatz Fosters. But Christ Church, Spitalfields – the gigantic Hawksmoor church which is perhaps the most striking Baroque religious building in Britain and was constructed between 1714 and 1729 as part of the High Church counterinsurgency campaign in stone which planned fifty new churches in the pagan slums – was until recently near derelict. Except for the recently renamed and refurbished Jack the Ripper, an ex-meths joint, most of

Dan Jones

Phil McCowan

Mrs Desai, leader of the strikers at Grunwick's film processing plant, Willesden, north London.

'Discontented native in the colonies, labour agitator in the mills, were the same serpent in alternative disguises.'

V. G. Keirnan

Brick Lane, made to measure.

the Lane's pubs retain their original names and layout.

The old gaunt tenement buildings in Fashion Street, Thrawl Street and Lowesworth Street reflected in their architecture the utilitarian aims of the charitable housing schemes erected for their improving effect on the morals and the work discipline of the *'deserving poor'*. They have now been largely replaced by courtyards of modern *vernacular* housing. There is no overall architectural style or period; a jerry-built minicab office butts into Georgian columns; a *West End* tailor's shop window layered in decades of honest dust is opposite a bright orange-neoned Indian sweet shop; on the corrugated iron, film posters, anti-racist propaganda and adverts for house clearance and karate clubs collide. The mosque, the London Jamme Masjid, which dominates the corner of Brick Lane and Fournier Street, was previously the Great Synagogue of the Jewish orthodox and before that the Huguenot Eglise

Clockwise above: Inside the Famous Clifton restaurant, 126 Brick Lane; The brewery chimney from Brick Lane; Two shops in Brick Lane.

Neuve. The sundial made by the French refugees and enscribed *1743 – Umbra Sumus* still crowns the apex of its pediment. And, on a smaller scale, the window display of B. Weinberg, Printer, tells a typographical history of migration, adaptation and assimilation in the notepaper printed for Minsky (Furs), Manchester and Bradford; Elegente Fashions, Berwick Street; the London Chess Conference (Chairman S. Rueben); the business cards of Labovitch the Glazier, who later becomes David Glassman and Family; and the change-of-address cards sent out for the move from Hackney to Woodford Green.

But if you half close your eyes you can still imagine it's the actors from the old Yiddish theatre at 3 Fournier Street planning their departure to New York at the next table of the Famous Clifton restaurant, that it's the anarchist-feminist Rose Witcop who is making all the noise in the queue for smoked-salmon bagels, and that it's Sylvia Pankhurst, the socialist suffragette, sprinting for the number 8 bus to take her to a *Worker's Dreadnought* editorial meeting in Bow. And then you look again and it's the contemporary heart-rending poverty you see and even the graffiti is misspelt: '**Fuk off Wogs**'.

The muddle is most magnificent during the Sunday market, known in the seventeenth century, when it began in Rosemary Lane, as the Rag Fair. Brick Lane market, with its little tributaries and subsections that trickle down the unmade side streets, is the most anarchic of London street markets. It was there that Malcolm McLaren, the manager-to-be of the Sex Pistols, used as a lad to sell 78 rpm records from a pushchair. Where else can you buy, off adjacent barrows, ballet tutus, second-hand teeth and toupees, Korean twist drills, rare Max Miller live recordings and a doll's house crammed with furniture?

Making ends meet, Brick Lane 1985.

The Sunday market is at the Bethnal Green end. Many of the Bengalis live and work in the opposite, Whitechapel section. But it would be quite wrong to see the dark railway bridge which bisects the lane as dividing the area into black and white sectors. There are white people, particularly of Irish and Jewish origin, who live and work throughout the street and the adjacent council estates. There has been very little Asian hostility towards them or the many people who come into the area to eat, shop and look. And although there is little private housing in the borough, Asian families whose first stop was Brick Lane now live throughout East London, including the prosperous settlements in Newham and Barking.

Judged by results, housing and transfer policy seems inept and some say corrupt and the Bengalis seem always to get slotted into the least desirable blocks in the vicinity. The problem here is that while the 'first come, first

Above: **Right To Work Campaign's Brixton office after a visit from the National Front.** Below: **Graffiti in Cheshire Street, Whitechapel.**

Syd Shelton

Nina Saunders

served' principle works perfectly well for a cab rank, it's unfair for the allocation of housing. What tends to happen is that migrant Londoners, new in the queue, get stuck on the very old cramped estates when what they desperately want is a bit of space for their young kiddies in three- or four-bedroom accommodation. But on the old estates their neighbours are likely to be either fellow migrants, with whom they may have nothing else in common, or *'problem'* families with bad debts, a police record, a tendency to violence and quite possibly gutter-racist leanings into the bargain. So in no time they are in some kind of ghastly parody of a concentration camp where the half-pissed skinhead camp commandant makes late-night patrols with a pack of Alsatians while the Asians imprison themselves behind barred windows. Dr Nazia Khanum, who now leads the GLC's race and housing team at Bow Road, prepared a detailed report on Bengali unemployment for the Tower Hamlets Adult Education Institute in 1983 which commented: **'When one sees the inevitable depression of a couple attempting to raise an ailing infant in such derelict hovels, it is hard to believe one is in the capital of a highly developed country.'** And everyone else treble-bolts the door and turns the TV up. This is no fun for anyone and the warmest heart in the world (and some of the long-standing tenants have them) can't build a spirit of neighbourliness out of a situation which everyone has a valid reason to resent.

There is also frequent intimidation and attacks against the Asians, especially on housing estates where they are new. According to the figures of the police, one in five of the indictable assaults in Tower Hamlets were on Asian victims, although Asians comprise barely a tenth of the population. The most recent GLC police monitoring figures show three times as many racist attacks reported to the police in East London as anywhere in the country. But the official response, if it was expressed at all, was couched in terms of the failings of the Asian people themselves; their substandard housing, their poor educational achievements, their employment difficulties and what could be done *'to help'*. There was a marked reluctance to listen, to open the official ear to complaints about the attacks by white racists, police indifference and the racial prejudice which could be smelt behind many of bureaucracies of local government. Indeed it would have been rather surprising if the governments and the officials who devoted so much zeal and ingenuity to keeping black people out of the country, and the police who showed such enthusiasm for passport checking and the *'fishing raids'* for *'illegals'* were then to show genuine concern for those people who, despite their efforts, had managed to settle.

The net result was such low confidence in the police in particular that people didn't bother to waste the time required to report incidents of racial attack. And the police, at least till the 1981 Home Office investigation and the reforms in police procedure that followed it, got a serious underestimate of the size of the problem and therefore an excuse to do less than they should. There had been abuse and attacks since the late sixties when among the little white thirteen- and fourteen-year-old squirts down the Commercial Road bashing an Asian elder off his bike was considered to be a sign of great bravery, but these were clearly worsening in scale and severity between 1976 and 1978. Alok Biswas wrote in the *Socialist Worker* in 1978: **'When I first came to this country in 1969 there was Paki-bashing. But it was never more than abuse. We could almost treat it as a joke. Then about two years ago it changed. The attacks became vicious. They meant to kill.'**

The evidence of Asian fear was all around. A *Warning: dog patrol* sign was stuck up by the Brick Lane mosque. In the evenings and the early mornings the tailors left the safety of Whitechapel in groups no smaller than three or four.

Pregnant women walked in groups to antenatal outpatient clinics at the London Hospital down Whitechapel Road. Minicab firms specialised in taking people to work and school, sometimes no more than four hundred yards. The Asian school kids at Stepney Green were let out of school early so that they would have time to get home unmolested. In Asian homes on council estates there were windows boarded up with hardboard or strung across with chicken wire.

By 1978 it had become impossible for anyone living or working in the E1 area not to have witnessed the provocations: doorstep and bus-stop abuse, the daubing of menacing graffiti, the window-breaking and air-gun pot shots, the stone and bottle-hurling sorties on Sundays, and the threatening atmosphere around certain estates and tube stations which produced a de facto curfew.

'On the first day of Christmas my true love gave t'me Roast fish and ackee.'
Jah Thomas

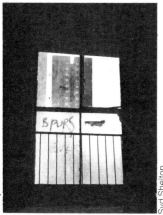

Andy Dark

Syd Shelton

Andy Dark

Andy Dark

Top left: **The view from Dennis House, Roman Road, Bow.** Top centre: **The Sandwich Bar, Hollybush Place, Bethnal Green Road.** Top right: **Gunmakers Lane, Bow.** Middle left: **Pultney Close, Bow.** Bottom right: **Jubilee Street, Stepney.**

One cannot accurately judge the degree to which these attacks were organised and co-ordinated. Some clearly were, others were a more random vandalism against a target which the popular press had encouraged the assailants to hate. For the thugs, violence was its own reward and racialism was useful to give that violence a political justification. But for the fascist tacticians active in the area – older men steeled and schooled in the street fighting of the Mosleyite revival – it became part of a calculated plan whose aim was to force the Asians to retaliate blindly. This, they hoped, would in turn force the whites to *'take sides'*, hopefully now with fascist leadership installed at their head. In this scheme they calculated on two tactical advantages. For

Syd Shelton

the kids who followed them – lumpen children of lumpen parents, physically belligerent, mentally bewildered, nursing a sense of betrayal by orthodox politics – Brick Lane was the perfect target: notorious, accessible and, so they thought, unlikely to offer serious resistance.

And the police were geared to preventing the community from defending itself (unnecessary, so they thought, and illegal anyway) and denied that what was being experienced by the Asians could possibly be taking place (because, at this stage, there was not a category on the police stationery in which it could be duly recorded). The net effect of this was also advantageous to the fascists in that it made the inhabitants of Brick Lane and their supporters more of a target for police attention than their attackers.

In the weeks after Altab Ali's murder, there were a series of attacks which clearly suggested co-ordination and organisation. On 27th June, Ishaque Ali died outside the LEB offices in Lower Clapton after three white men chanted 'Paki bastards' and 'stinking blacks' at him and his brother Faquruddin and then attacked them, choking Ishaque with a bootlace. He left four children. His brother's life was only saved by the intervention of an unknown, heroic passing West Indian who stopped his car and chased the assailants away. On 6th July a group of Asian brewery workers were ambushed as they left the evening shift at Bass Charrington's bottling plant in Three Mills Lane, Bow. A convoy of six cars halted to disgorge thirty men who pelted them with bricks and bottles in a concerted volley. Eight had to go to hospital, two were admitted, but the police still insisted it was not a racial attack.

In Brick Lane itself, the pitch where the National Front news and fascist pamphlets were hawked was reinforced in numbers and in hostility. The Trades Council logged a total of thirty-four serious incidents in the first eight months of 1978, the most brazen on Sunday 11th June when a full-scale window-smashing mob, some 150 strong, was mobilised from all over London and attempted to charge the length of the Lane. The squadron had assembled openly after a Front street meeting and included youths bussed in from as far afield as Peckham, Dagenham, Putney and South Ockenden, and directed by known local fascists. They succeeded in breaking a few windows and car windscreens and knocking a fifty-five-year-old shopkeeper unconscious before they were chased off. It was an ominous echo of the Kristallnacht when the Nazi Party started public attacks on the shops of Jews in Germany. But considering that this surprise attack was launched after the police and the Left had gone home from the demonstrations, which now took place every Sunday, it was a tactical failure. Rahmin Ali wrote of the scene:

At that time Brick Lane was nearly empty since by then most people had gone home for lunch, and I felt that these young thugs would smash up every Asian shop in the Lane – I was horrified to think how many innocent Asian people would become the victims of these armed racists. But to my great joy and astonishment, I saw within a couple of minutes over fifteen Asian youths get together, standing firmly to defend their community. Then a few more joined the battle to defend Brick Lane. The racist thugs were taken by surprise. They thought that the Asians were

Fascist newspaper sellers.

John Sturrock (Network)

'I got a plate in front of me but nothing that's on it. Because all of us are sitting at the same table, are all of us diners? I'm not a diner until you let me dine.'
Malcolm X

Brick Lane, Sunday 11th June 1978, 3 pm.

Dan Jones

Shops in Brick Lane.

cowed, and that it would only be a few minutes before they could wave their union jacks down Brick Lane. THEY WERE WRONG. Asian youths know well how to defend themselves. Faced with this strength and courage the racists had no option but to run back to where they had come from.

For what had not been considered by the fascists and what proved the decisive element in the next few weeks was the political mood of the Asians of E1 themselves. The first gathering at the Queen's Hall back in 1971, after the skinhead murder of Mr T. Ali who worked in a Wimpy Bar, had been a meeting of fear: chaotic, imploring, literally praying for help, weakly organised by old men. By 1976 (and after a war of independence for Bangladesh in 1971 in which one million died and the Syleti people began to feel quite different about themselves), they were here to stay and to fight if necessary. Although a great meeting at the Naz Cinema in 1976 marched anticlimactically off to the Leman Street police station protesting at the police failure to deal with racist attacks, the teenage boys in the audience had been soaking up the cadences of Darcus Howe, the Trinidad-born editor of *Race Today*, who prowled the platform, snarling lucid defiance, superbly sending up the worthies on the stage and insisting, with every pore of his being, that the black communities, Asian and Afro-Caribbean, must set their own agendas, command their own organisations and to their own selves be true. It was at this meeting that the *Self-defence is no offence* slogan, so important in outer East London in the eighties, originated.

And it was these lads: bright, inquiring, failing at school because of language problems which the teachers couldn't handle, true scallywags in the East End tradition, who were working out their ideas between 1976 and 1979 in what had become a virtual college of the streets. Listening to the *Race Today* crew, to Shah Lutfur Rahman, then secretary of the Bangladeshi Welfare Association, barrister, drama teacher and socialist of great culture, hammering away at *Mr Dan* (Dan Jones, the secretary of the Trades Council), listening and reading with a mixture of horror and fascination the newspapers and leaflets of the Socialist Workers Party and arguing, incessantly, with each other about tactics, about politics and about their patriarchal uncles who still ran the clothing factories, the restaurants and the mosque. Learning their politics as they went along. Working out that they had to get a response from the devout old men of the mosque. And that there was great danger in isolating themselves in melodramatic gestures. But anticipating that the elders would think the answer was being nice to Peter Shore or the bishop or the leader of the council, without really doing anything or challenging anyone. So learning both to work with them and to challenge them. And sussing out which socialist suitors could offer more than hot air and membership forms and beginning to wonder about how to operate within a trade-union structure which sometimes seemed designed never to make a decision.

What is remarkable in this process is the success of the hard-pressed migrants in survival, organisation and growth in a harsh environment. The achievement of the Asians in finding their feet and, in the process, a new identity is no less formidable than that of the earlier Jewish migration, which took from Rudolph Rocker to Arnold Wesker's Auntie Sadie or from the 1889 dock strike to the battle of Cable Street – that is three full generations – to find their cockney footing. The older Sikhs, who have often had educational and military experience under the British Raj, are, with their turbans and their walking sticks, now a recognised feature of East London life and have been for at least thirty years. The African Asians who took refuge here from Amin's Ugandan persecutions and from Africanisation in Kenya and Malawi were often educated and self-assured traders. But the cultural journey made by the Bengalis from the family farms of northeast Bangladesh to the hard life of piecework in the East End rag trade has catapulted them from the rich paddyfields and seasonal floods of rural Sylhet to the hard streets and fast cars of one of the biggest cities in the world.

In the countryside of Bangladesh, Islamic traditions are dominant, the family structure is devoutly patriarchal, marriages are 'arranged' and purdah still operates. The patterns of belief, family and sexual mores are those of a rural society not yet pulverised and reassembled by the shock waves of industrialisation. Their position is more like that of the Jewish fugitives from the *stetls* and *mirs* of Poland and the steppes a century ago. The intensity of the

British Movement skins, Aldgate.

Syd Shelton

'Nationalism continues to appeal to the depleted because other prospects appear bleaker.'

Freddy Perlman

Improved Dwellings, Stepney.

political forcing experience that the youth in that community are going through is enormous. The radicalisation of the self-defence movement leads some to begin to scrutinise the conservatism of their own community, the authority of their elders, the relevance of their faith, the position of women. They are having to learn to deal with the mainly white Left, with the police and with other sometimes unsympathetic minorities. We do not yet know the identity of the Bengali Bronowski, the Sikh Wesker or the Pakistani Mikardo, but they will come. Ken Leech is probably right to suggest that '**the emergence of a new Bengali radicalism is the most encouraging and the most hopeful aspect of the whole period . . . The ghetto has produced not despair and resignation but anger and organised revolt.**' It is tempting to compare them with the defiant young Jewish rebels who organised the anarchist Freedom Club in Brick Lane before the First World War, rejected marriage for *free union* and defied the authority of Tory Anglo-Jewry by brandishing bacon sandwiches and lighted cigarettes as the orthodox left the Great Synagogue of Fournier Street on Yom Kippur.

But for all the talk, the young Bengali men are deeply conservative, profoundly steeped in Sylheti tradition, respect for elder brother, stranglehold of the extended family and the subordination of women. If young people isolate themselves from their community, by their politics, their tactics or their friends, they risk becoming powerless. In Dan Jones's view, '**This may change for the brown cockneys born here now of Bengali parents, but it honestly hasn't really for the class of '78. These are deep-down values, hung on to sometimes more fiercely here than back in Sylhet.**' One must also remember the historian's verdict on the intense conservatism of orthodox Jewry, '**in the face of a dark reality, they chose to live in the past**', and recall that in the Renaissance, the Jews dressed almost mediaevally, and in the nineteenth century they still sported the ruffs and wigs of the Renaissance. Is the elaborate, coded beauty of the sari speaking the same, eloquent, wordless disdain for the leather miniskirt and stiletto heels manufactured in adjacent workshops of E1?

Because of the political maturity of this young settlement, what the NF wanted, street fighting between black and white in E1, did not occur. There were no Bengali race riots, revenge bombings or counterassassinations. Instead the Spitalfields Asians responded with firm dignity, firm militancy and a new-found unity. And their long-standing local white allies from the socialist groups, the Tower Hamlets Trades Council and the local churches in the immediate area were supplemented by a wider range of whites prepared to challenge the racists' right to speak for East London opinion.

It was a local initiative which proved decisive in turning the tide in the East End: the audacious call by the Hackney and Tower Hamlets Defence Committee for a Black Solidarity day on Monday 17th July 1978. It was more of a stay at home than a strike in many ways, a mixture of defence, respect and defiance, and involved over 8000 people, ranging from body-plant workers in Ford's Dagenham car plant and rag-trade workers throughout the borough to the shop and restaurant owners. The strike was supported by some whites directly concerned with the issues of racism in schools and local government, and many school students.

Any token strike is a matter of demonstration of opinion rather than the application of power, especially one with a relatively narrow union base. There had, for example, not been time or machinery properly to involve the

'I would hurl words into this darkness and wait for an echo; and if an echo sounded, no matter how faintly, I would send other words to tell, to march, to fight, to create a sense of the hunger for life that gnaws in us all, to keep alive in our hearts a sense of the inexpressively human.'
Richard Wright

The Solidarity March leaves Brick Lane in the strike against racial attacks which closed shops, businesses and schools throughout East London on 17th July 1978.

Shops in Brick Lane.

transport and hospital unions, where black workers have a well-established presence in London, but it is significant that the link and response were not there. And there was not, even at this stage, the automatic *'black solidarity'* which the platform speakers like to conjure up – most Afro-Caribbeans did not identify with the Brick Lane issue. But, as Alok Biswas wrote the following week,

The impact of the anti-racist strike has touched many thousands of black workers up and down the country but it has a special meaning for the Bengali people who live in East London's Spitalfields. The whole area is bubbling with enthusiasm and determination to continue the struggle. What I saw this weekend was a whole community expressing itself against injustice, privilege and oppression.

And Shuel Uddin, one of the many Asian T & G shop stewards in Ford's, Dagenham, drew attention in the *Socialist Worker* to the backing of 'white workers coming out as well and many more supporting our action'.

An incident on the day made the point better than the flashy orators and radical movies screened in the Naz Cinema. As a massive, ebullient and mainly male crowd surged down Bethnal Green Road, a trio of yobbos yelled abuse from a car. The police arrested two Bengali boys who shouted back at them and a white marcher who tried to help. The provocateurs mysteriously got away. The incident symbolised exactly the attitude the strike and march were called to repudiate. The police had done it again. So the whole march just sat down, blocking Bethnal Green Road for half a mile back from the nick in an improvised street party, singing, shouting and speech-making in the sunshine, until the police released their prisoners.

I was returning to the surgery after a long batch of home visits and witnessed a panic-stricken senior policeman who was trying to seal off Bethnal Green Road under the bridge, by the Salmon and Ball, the pub outside which Oswald Mosley's British Union of Fascists held their street meetings in the thirties. For years the railway bridge had been the site of a graffiti battle between the racists and the Left, people hanging upside down in turn to overpaint each other's slogans. After about a quarter-inch of paint, the National Front gave up. But today the racists got their real answer.

An old Polish Jew said to me outside the chemist, quietly but with a voice that had seen a century, **'So the Swartzers mean business at last.'** We had all sensed it: the birth of a new sort of power. Poor Altab Ali had his memorial after all. And it was better than bricks and mortar.

'Enoch Powell has predicted race riots in this country by 1986. For completely different reasons I see violent expressions of our position in and disgust with white society some years before them.'
Chris Mullard

WHAT'S GOING ON?

Widen the focus. Put the events in East London into the national political melodrama. Apart from numerous prologues, speeches and scenes off, the three main actors are the migrant communities, the active Left and the fascists.

First, the communities. The main events in Brick Lane (racism, resistance and political renaissance) have also occurred, with differing ingredients and timings, in Brixton, Liverpool 8, Southall, Bristol, Swansea and half a dozen more British towns. Indeed sparks like these have flown right across Western Europe as migrant workers unexpectedly took the lead: Turks in the waves of unofficial strikes in West Germany, North Africans in the Renault production lines outside Paris, and young Moluccans fighting back against racists in the streets of Rotterdam. And each is a single molten ember from a social forge: the immense proletarianisation which has drawn into the capitalist metropolises the ex-slaves, ex-coolies and ex-peasants of their erstwhile colonies and conquests, in a process which is nothing less than the remaking of the West European working class.

In the fifties the first generation of black migrants to Britain were invited, sometimes enticed and usually welcomed, as long as they worked diligently, didn't complain and made their own arrangements for the rest of their lives. New arrivals were empirically exploited not only by indigenous employers, landlords and estate agents but by unscrupulous fellows. There was occasional violent animosity. The settlers were crowded into what is now called the inner city because of the reluctance of white Britons to rent them accommodation elsewhere. And, largely unremarked upon, informal discrimination (*'the done thing'*) put clear limits on what black Britons were permitted to attain or even aspire to, with the possible exception of the bloody democracy of the boxing ring. But in Ladbroke Grove, Lambeth, St Anne's, Manningly, Moss Side and Chapeltown, the black settlers grinned and cursed and swallowed their pride and stuck it out.

But their British children have grown up, rightly expecting something better. Born British, educated, talking pungent street slang and our rich regional dialects as well as their parents' language; not prepared to apologise for their existence, to kowtow to officialdom, to dress respectably, deferentially and drably. It is a matter of attitude rather than formal politics, has involved painful battles with the authorities in school, on the streets and in the prisons and has occasionally taken forms destructive to fellow proletarians. It is perhaps best heard rather than read: at the thunderous dub stations and steel-band ramps

Jamaican workers arriving in Tilbury on the *Empire Windrush* in 1948. 492 men alighted and within three weeks it was reported: '76 have gone to work in foundries, 15 on the railways, 15 as labourers, 15 as farm workers, and ten as electricians. The others have gone into a wide variety of jobs, including the Post Office, coachbuilding and plumbing.'

Popperfoto

of the Notting Hill Carnival, in the poetic idioms of the prophetic and often tragic voices of the Black Power movement and the oratory of the rank-and-file strike leaders from Indian and Pakistani origins in Britain, and in the self-confident syntheses of music like Steel Pulse's *Handsworth Revolution*, a Brumification of Rasta militancy, and the Bangladeshi band Disharhi who have brought the spirit of the revolutionary poet Kobi Nazrul to trade unionism in East London. It is an attitude of clear-headed and dignified defiance which has proved contagious and inspiring to whites who also rebel against the banal certainties of modern capitalism. And it is this new spirit which worries bourgeois politicians, Brylcreemed police chiefs and tense-waisted civil servants.

Darcus Howe, an editor of *Race Today*, put the change that has taken place plainly in a speech in Bradford in the late seventies. After an account of his humiliation in his first job in Britain, as a postal sorter in Mount Pleasant, a Bunyanesque railway-station quarter of London, he asserted that the present black community 'is no longer willing to live in the room, traipse after the police, do the employers' bidding so they can create their wealth. We are no longer that defeated, demoralised working class. And *that* is that which the authorities are compelled to attack.'

If the British-born blacks were on the ascendant in the mid-seventies, the fortunes of the Left of 1968 vintage were entering a prolonged eclipse. Between 1968 and 1974 in Britain there had been a rising arc of labour unrest without parallel since the twenties. It had not simply been a struggle about wages and conditions but questioned the authority of the employers and the legitimacy of the government. A new political agenda of feminism, workers' control, rock and roll and republicanism was being perused by workers in the hospital wards, offices, shipyards and car factories, from Aberdeen to Derry, imaginatively advocated by a socialist and underground press which had, in total, a readership of hundreds of thousands. The ideals and the idealism of the insurgent student movement fed into an upward swing of unofficial and often illegal trade-union activity. As the labour historian Royden Harrison writes, the strikes of the National Union of Mineworkers in 1972 and 1974

'The National Front put me on the cover of their magazine and called me an albino nigger – excellent praise.'
John Lydon

first blew the Government *off course*: then they landed it on the rocks. First they compelled the Prime Minister to receive them in No. 10 and forced him to concede more in twenty-four hours than had been conceded in the last twenty-four years. Then two years later their strike led him to introduce the three-day week – a novel form of government by catastrophe – for which he was rewarded with defeat at the General Election.

Harold Wilson came back to replace Heath as prime minister in February 1974. He and the trade union leaders tried to consolidate gains cautiously in the face of the recession triggered by the oil crisis. The insurgent industrial movement faltered: strike days in 1974 were 13 million, in 1975 only 5 million. Unemployment began to rise.

Unknown

Student revolutionaries storm the American Embassy in Grosvenor Sq, Mayfair, in solidarity with the National Liberation Front of Vietnam, March 1967.

It was only too easy for the lightweight crafts of the groups on the Left to become disorientated in the sudden crosscurrents and violent political eddies of this period. In Britain a veritable flotilla of political groups had embarked in the late sixties on the revolutionary voyage. But by 1975 quite a few had capsized, collided or turned back. Among the rest there was a good deal of gesticulation, whether in signal or in distress was not entirely clear, and noisy but implausible proclamations of autonomy and buoyancy. But even on the best equipped of the little convoy, the SS *International Socialism*, negligent map reading and overoptimistic meteorological forecasting were commonplace. From the prow of our vessel, things still looked very promising. The political climate, if temporarily overcast, would soon brighten, our crew

'Restoring order' during the building workers' strike of 1972.

was still growing in size and despite slackening of overall progress, we were pulling away from our immediate rivals. Ahead was the great lopsided bulk of HMS *Labour Party*, its legislative propellers, only half in the water, churning the social-democratic liner in ever decreasing circles. The captain had difficulty retaining control of the wheel, there were arguments in the officers' mess, and the stewards' reassurances to the restive passengers were obviously bogus. It was surely only a matter of time before those on board who genuinely wished to get to the socialist destination jumped ship and joined us. In our enthusiasm, we failed to notice the *battle-grey fleet of Thatcher* which, in the middle distance, was already slipping into the underwater formation that would, in 1979, Belgrano us all.

At the time, whatever the state of our engine room and the quality of our charts, it had to be full steam ahead. We knew that in uncharted waters,

'The universe is checkin' us out. Historically we have come from the age of ignorance, through the age of enlightenment, to the age of arrogance. That's where we're at now on the cosmic scale. But if we don't get our shit together on the mundane plane, we'll never fly, we'll all die, in the bye and bye and the last question will be, why?'
Jalal Uridin

37

underwater obstacles are the principal hazard. But no one could have predicted there would be quite so many rocks, storms and torpedoes ahead.

In January 1977, our group's name was changed from the International Socialists, which had served since 1962, to the Socialist Workers Party. Despite a membership of only 4000, we launched a national Right to Work campaign (note the optimistic mood, no plaintive appeal to *save* jobs), contested parliamentary by-elections, published a monthly campaigning magazine of proletarian feminism, and had near weekly trials of strength with the National Front in marches, pickets and counterdemonstrations across Britain.

For the primary political beneficiary of the palsied performance of the Labour Party in those years of impasse between 1974 and the decisive deflation on terms dictated by the International Monetary Fund of 1978 was not, as we had hoped, the independent socialist groupings to the left of Labour but the fascist far Right.

> 'Mrs Thatcher's always talking about the Falklands spirit. I think the trouble with this country is that there's a lot of Belgrano spirit — hurray for me, fuck you.'
> **Tony Merchant**

The National Front had been formed in February 1967 by a merger of traditional anti-Semitic, fascist and nationalist sects. But apart from some significant but short-winded activity in support of Enoch Powell in 1968, it had remained a marginal force. The Front ran only ten candidates in the 1970 general election and all did very badly. Their breakthrough came in May 1973 in the aftermath of the Ugandan Asian crisis when a then unknown National Front organiser called Martin Webster won 4789 votes in the West Bromwich by-election and saved his deposit. And while the fifty or so NF candidates in the two general elections of 1974 again did poorly (with exceptions in Wolverhampton, Leicester and East London), the total vote, scale and financing of the operation was alarming. When Asians seeking refuge from Africanisation in Malawi started to arrive at Gatwick airport in the summer of 1976, the Front, supported by the popular press, campaigned vigorously against giving them refuge. Racism was getting so respectable that no fewer than 3225 (6.6 per cent) of the electorate in the comfortable Thames Estuary constituency of Thurrock voted NF in June 1976, either not knowing or not caring that they were being conned by a bunch of Nazis.

Junior fascists in Hoxton, 1976.

The Front's political progress was possible because official and legal attitudes echoed their prejudices in a more polite idiom. The 'moderate' consensus in the debate was now in favour of tightening immigration controls based on a colour bar and associated legislation which would produce the 1982 Nationality Act with its three, unequal classes of citizenship. A series of individually plausible migration measures made Heathrow one of the most feared entry points in Europe with a cramped detention centre, forced interrogation, bone X-rays to check age, virginity tests and various forms of trick questioning and entrapment becoming common practice. In British embassies abroad, it was officially confirmed in 1985, officials dealing with entry-certificate clearance hold up the families and dependants of successful settlers endlessly in their country of origin on a racial basis. Migrants who get past all this are still subject, once in Britain, to random passport checks, *'fishing raids'* at factories and lodging houses, and even identity clearance when they go to see a hospital doctor.

The debate centred on immigration controls but had implications for the civil rights of migrants who had quite legally settled. A generation of people who had, literally, made Britain what it is were suddenly getting cold stares from their neighbours, being asked to justify their existence by officials and forced to guard their lives from the fascists.

Margaret Thatcher caught the mood perfectly by accosting a black mother in the streets of South London and inquiring querulously, '**Now, which part of**

John Sturrock (Network)

Africa do you come from?'

'Tooting,' she was told.

With this sort of respectable backing the NF was able to break out of the political small time and address and attract a wider and younger audience. Now when you peered through the police cordon, there was an altered NF; the obvious nutters were outnumbered by men and some women and children who were genuine political recruits. At an estimate, the NF's total paid-up membership in this period was 17,000 (some 7000 larger than the highest total recorded by the British Union of Fascists) and it was producing 5 or 6 million items of printed propaganda per year.

The NF were no longer an abstract threat to their targets. They were increasingly bold in leading marches into suburbs with a high proportion of immigrant residents. I can vividly remember an NF outing of this period which ended an election meeting in Hoxton. What stays in the memory is not the formidable show of opposition in Bethnal Green itself, the banners against the NF held by the nurses, ancillary staff and doctors on the steps of the Queen Elizabeth II Children's Hospital in the Hackney Road, or even the bravery of the teenagers who ducked the police escort and sprinted down back streets to show their anger face to face. The memory is a momentary glimpse of a West Indian mother at a third-floor Shoreditch council window pulling her kids away from their viewpoint. The children must have thought it was some kind of celebration, with the flags and drums and excitement. The mother knew the truth and tried to hide it from them. Neither of us realised that round the corner the National Front *stewards* were taking iron bars and cudgels to counter-demonstrators. The police, however, did. And sat in their Transit vans watching impassively.

It would, of course, be inaccurate to suggest that concern about racism and the rise of the National Front was confined to the members of the socialist groups to the left of the Labour Party. An older generation, schooled in the battles against Oswald Mosley's British Union of Fascists in the thirties but now in positions of influence in the trade unions and the Labour Party, had kept a watching brief for decades. The '43 Group, a left-wing committee of Jewish ex-servicemen and women, had existed since the end of the Second World War publishing the newsletter *On Guard*. It later developed into the '62 Group, a well-organised anti-fascist vigilante. The Jewish Board of Deputies Defence Committee kept a constant and well-informed watch on the fascist groups, and the anti-fascist periodical *Searchlight*, founded by Gerry Gable, Reg Freeson and Joan Lestor in 1964, operated a sophisticated intelligence system on tiny resources. At the Institute of Race Relations, liberated from its refined Establishment origins in the West End and transported to King's Cross, Sivanandan and other black intellectuals pored over press cuttings, economic analyses and an Aladdin's cave of political literature and periodicals. The race-relations industry, that is, projects to monitor and improve race relations financed by government, grew rapidly.

It would also be unfair to dismiss the work done by white people in various local anti-racist committees, the Community Relations Officers, the Joint Councils for the Welfare of Immigrants, trade unionists who had continued anti-colonial traditions, church people, lawyers, teachers and journalists who insisted on taking sides, often to their personal cost. Yet they did not amount to a national force and they were not effectively organised to respond to the National Front's advance. In the words of Ann Dummett's sober account of this period in the epilogue of *A Portrait of English Racism*,

Junior fascist in Berlin, 1932.

Enoch Powell.

'Often when I am kneeling down in church, I think to myself how much we should thank God, the Holy Ghost, for the gift of capitalism.'
Enoch Powell

the number of people actively concerned about racism had increased from very small indeed to small. The number of white people uneasily aware that it existed in the country, and was itself a serious problem, increased considerably but their awareness was often still confused and inadequately informed and not very fruitful of results.

Ironically, the National Front changed this. For black people the electoral support for the NF wasn't at all surprising and the inhumanity of racism wasn't exactly hot news either. There are blacks who prefer the NF's open racism to the hypocrites in the Labour and Tory parties who think pretty much the same but disguise it. The everyday insults and officially enshrined prejudices were more important than small electoral votes for minority parties who frankly espoused a racism which was everywhere anyway. But the NF's rising vote, over 100,000 in Greater London in 1976, their greater confidence in public and the insistent graffiti which defaced the streets in every inner city in Britain, obliged white people to consider an organised reply. Yet counterdemonstration, the most obvious response, did not prove decisive, and to the average observer sometimes gave the unfortunate impression of two bunches of nutters pursuing a private quarrel.

It is intriguing that the first initiative to form a quite new sort of anti-fascist organisation came from an off-the-wall bunch of left-wing arties outside the leadership of any of the established organisations. In August 1976, Eric Clapton, the blues guitarist who had made a fortune out of black music, including a highly lucrative cover version of Bob Marley's reggae classic *I Shot The Sheriff*, interrupted a Birmingham concert to make a rambling speech in support of Enoch Powell, the MP most associated with open opposition to black Britons. Red Saunders, a photographer with long experience on the Left and an unrepentant ex-mod, composed an instant letter of protest and got it signed (over the phone) by six friends:

When we read about Eric Clapton's Birmingham concert when he urged support for Enoch Powell, we nearly puked. Come on Eric . . . you've been taking too much of that *Daily Express* stuff and you know you can't handle it. Own up. Half your music is black. You're rock music's biggest colonist. You're a good musician but where would you be without the blues and R & B? You've got to fight the racist poison otherwise you degenerate into the sewer with the rats and all the money men who ripped off rock culture with their cheque books and plastic crap. We want to organise a rank and file movement against the racist poison in music. We urge support for Rock against Racism. P.S. Who shot the Sheriff Eric? It sure as hell wasn't you!

It was published by the *New Musical Express*, *Melody Maker* and *Sounds*, the three main pop-music weeklies at the time, and the *Socialist Worker*. It's easy to find the sixties hip talk a little dated now, yet a sense of outrage came across and there was an address to write to. And people did write, many long and passionate letters, over 140 in the first week, all enthusiastic. Rock Against Racism had been born and was wailing lustily.

Clapton was not the only musician coming out with this garbage. Also in

Portobello Road, Notting Hill Gate, 1957.

1976 David Bowie told a *Playboy* interviewer of his sympathy with fascism, which he rightly defined as 'a very extreme form of nationalism', and staged a Nazi-style return to Victoria station with Mercedes limousine, outriders and salutes which chillingly mixed rock-star megalomania with Third Reich references. (A biography by his first manager, David Pitt, claims that Bowie's parents had been briefly involved with Mosley's Union Movement.) But although Bowie subsequently, 'after a real ticking off by some Berlin socialists', made a complete retraction of his coked-up Nazi flirtation, he was reflecting a real enough mood. 'It was that hideous thing where as an artist you kind of feel there's something in the air,' he recalled in 1983. 'I can't put it any

© Keith Silva

41

Red Saunders

Syd Shelton

Syd Shelton · Klad McNulty

other way, but you can just feel it, you just sense a situation or an atmosphere and that can go into your writing.'

Yet Eric Clapton announced to the *Melody Maker*, to the further horror of his fellow blues lovers, that Enoch Powell 'was the only bloke who was telling the truth, for the good of the country'. RAR had to get organised.

Socialist Worker had loaned RAR its address in Shoreditch (which was promptly petrol-bombed by the Nazi group Column 88) and gave a page of the paper over to printing some of the replies. RAR's next step was to organise our own concert.

If RAR was to present cultural shows to combat the NF's influence on people's minds, the ideas had to be in all-night day-glo, not just a little diatribe popped in between the music. The obvious idea in those days was a pub gig. The East End was chosen because that was where the National Front still

'I don't think anybody steals anything: all of us borrow.'
B. B. King

Montage: Andy Dark

Top: *Temporary Hoarding*, issue No. 7. Middle: **Women punks, West Runton posse.** Bottom left: **Barry Forde.**

Bottom right: **John Cooper Clarke.** Middle right *(l-r):* **Elvis Presley, Chuck Berry, Little Richard, Jerry Lee Lewis.**

claimed they were strong, and a pub called the Princess Alice in Forest Gate was booked for November 1976. Roger Huddle had seen Carol Grimes at the Hope and Anchor in Islington and thought she was not only a great singer but playing RAR's kind of music. She understood what Rock Against Racism was immediately. She loathed racism, lived in Bethnal Green with her son, came from a black music tradition and, although she was one of the best blues singers in Britain, never got anywhere with the record companies because she refused to be prettied up and sold like a shampoo that could sing.

Security had to be reliable and the Royal Group of Docks Shop Stewards Committee were recruited to provide it. The dockers at first were unconvinced about RAR – 'No, it will never happen' – but arrived all right on the night with a bulky Adidas bag saying 'Not to worry, the tools are here.'

It was a success, not just packed out and a great atmosphere, but highly political in quite a new way. There was one East End racist in the audience who happened to like Carol Grimes. There he was enjoying himself but there was a big banner up saying *Black and White Unite* and stickers and leaflets asking *What are we going to do about the NF?* He was up to the neck in left-wing ideas but having a good time. Wilhelm Reich, the avant-garde German psychiatrist who diagnosed as a fatal weakness in the German Left's opposition to Hitler its refusal to take seriously the cultural and sexual dimensions of fascism's appeal, would have loved it.

It took to the end of 1976 for the little RAR group to hammer out its ideas and consolidate a core of visual artists, musicians and writers who could drive the project ahead. But for that group the feeling of fear and passivity against the Front's advance was over, at least in our heads; we were going to strike back kung-fu, rub-a-dub, surrealist style. RAR's resources were small and we still participated in our other personas as committed lefties in the direct confrontations with the National Front. It was a piece of double time, with the musical and the political confrontations on simultaneous but separate tracks and difficult to mix. The music came first and was more exciting. It provided the creative energy and the focus in what became a battle for the soul of young working-class England. But the direct confrontations and the hard-headed political organisation which underpinned them were decisive.

The NF's first big demonstration of 1977 was planned for April, through a multi-cultured inner city suburb where long-standing Jewish and Irish citizens had been joined by post-war migrants from the Caribbean, Cyprus, India and Pakistan: Wood Green. A loose alliance of political and ethnic groups including the local Labour and Communist parties united to oppose the Wood Green march. But there was considerable disagreement about tactics, with the leadership of the Labour Party and the Communist Party and the official ethnic bodies concentrating on pressure to get the march banned while they held a separate protest rally. The SWP led the argument for direct confrontation which was not, as a North London SWP organiser recalls, at all easy:

Although the position is won now, before the Anti-Nazi League, on the question of confrontation in the streets, we were in a tiny minority. But because we were extremely cocky, many people would say over-cocky, we absolutely went for that position and we

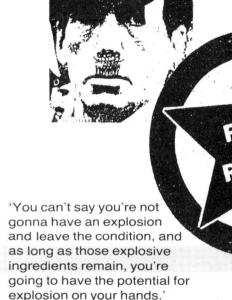

Paper of the Anti-Racist, Anti-Fascist Co-ordinating Committee.

'You can't say you're not gonna have an explosion and leave the condition, and as long as those explosive ingredients remain, you're going to have the potential for explosion on your hands.'
Malcolm X

43

pulled people. Partly because people didn't want to miss any excitement, a lot of that, and also because we were quite clearly the best organised. We always had the leaflets out first, we knew the terrain and we knew where we were going. It's a very good example of the old adage about giving the decisive lead in favourable circumstance and people will come with you.

So while the worthies addressed a rather small audience in a local park, the Front and their police protectors were faced with much more numerous, better organised and determined opposition armed with smoke bombs, flares, bricks, bottles and planned ambushes. At Ducketts Corner, where the previous year the anti-NF forces would probably have been content to jeer, there was a spontaneous move to block the road and physically attack the Front. Those arrested, including Ruth Gregory, a graphic artist in the RAR group, did not go quietly. Conventional anti-fascist politicos had been augmented by North London tribal gangs, rockabillies, soul girls and tracksuited Rastas checking out the platform oratory and suddenly executing fast sallies into the ranks of flabbergasted Front marchers, who especially hated the

'The thinking process, as your Honour well knows, is a process that defies jailing.'
Claudia Jones

racially mixed-up style-gangs and the monkey-booted all-women posses. A batch of dogged student lefties stoically chanting 'The National Front is a Nazi Front' were shocked into silence by the sight of a squad of black kids accurately hurling training shoes borrowed from Freeman, Hardy and Willis

Ducketts Corner, Wood Green.

44

street-display buckets. A smoke-bomb barrage obliterated the honour guard's spiked Union Jacks and for a moment the police line weakened and it looked as if they would not pass.

Not only were the NF marchers reduced to an ill-organised and bedraggled queue but there was extensive evidence of local dislike for the unwanted march and the trouble it had brought.

The argument over tactics was repeated in the run-up to the Front's next major effort, an August 1977 *'anti-mugging'* march in South London, between New Cross and Lewisham Town Hall, where a high proportion of Afro-Caribbean and Mediterranean residents coexisted with a relatively high fascist vote in local elections. This was the turning point. The word was out across London: something was going to happen. The opponents of confrontation (such as the Communist Party) possessed only one argument: organised action by the committed was no substitute for understanding by the multitude. Our reply was that popular support had to be won, somehow wrenched away from ignorance and prejudice and the stupidities of the mass media, by the direct action of an initially small nucleus of organised individuals. Socialist tactical writing is full of heroic images for this process: sparks setting alight prairie fires and small motors starting big engines. But in fact the process is really much more like political gardening; the putting down of good seeds, the rooting and grafting of ideas, the mixture of judgement and experience, inspiration and plain luck which can produce its harvest of fruit and flowers.

The SWP organisers held detailed meetings to brief delegates from all its London districts, arranged legal backup and provided a detailed street map. Although the police located and broke into the operation headquarters early on the day of the march, stewards had been assigned their final points on the route and the plans were passed by word of mouth.

By this time the momentum was so great that the NF march would have been physically attacked even if the police had arrested every SWP member in London. For the long history of attempted local fascist activity in South London guaranteed well-established anti-fascist local groupings, of various political flavours and sophisticated organisation, among the black communities. There had also been much discussion, initiated by South London black women, about racism in the women's movement and the need for feminists to oppose the National Front. National coordination of local anti-fascist groups had improved and a visually imaginative coordinating newspaper, *CARF*, Campaign Against Racism and Fascism, was in production.

The incoming Commissioner of the Metropolitan Police, David McNee, inflamed passions further by refusing to ban the NF march through Lewisham in a way that made it seem almost as though he regarded the issue as being the ability of his men to protect the fascists rather than defend the local population.

On the morning of the march, Lewisham shopping centre saw the now familiar scene of noisy boarding-up of shop fronts. The *official* protest march, including the Catholics, the councillors and the Communists, made indignant speeches against fascism in Lewisham and carefully avoided going within two miles of the fascists who were assembling behind the British Rail station at New Cross where the atmosphere was less forgiving. As a group of NFers left New Cross station, I saw a young East London comrade just pick up a brick and lob it at them, very coldly.

In New Cross Road, just down from Goldsmiths' College, a crowd of 5000 anti-NFers had assembled by midday. People gently milled; here surging

'Without struggle there is no progress. And those who profess to favour freedom yet depreciate agitation are men who want crops without digging up the ground and the ocean without the awful roar of its waters.'

Frederick Douglas

45

forward under banners that sprang and swooped like kites, there breaking out into feminist war whoops, elsewhere shouting recognition in noisy South London patois. In different idioms, everyone pressed towards Clifton Rise. At the front, a ram-packed contingent of South London Afro-Caribbeans cordially but expertly blocked off the police's first attempts – uphill and on foot – to open a way for the NF procession. Up on a traffic bollard a Trinidadian giant with a hand megaphone was thoughtfully advising the crowd, rather as a cricket captain might place his field, and, in the lulls, making speeches.

So when the police finally succeeded in opening a passage for the NF march down New Cross Road an hour and a half after the scheduled start, it was done with more brutality than finesse. As the police prepared their charge, an Afro-Caribbean woman who had been watching from the top floor of her home hoisted her hi-fi speaker onto her windowsill. It was playing Bob

Below: **The NF march fails to get started, for the third time, at Clifton Rise, New Cross.**
Right: **New Cross Rd, Lewisham.**

Marley, *Get up, stand up . . .* Almost directly opposite her a Cypriot woman replied with a clenched-fist salute from the first floor of her boarded-up kebab-and-chips shop. Two minutes later an officer with a megaphone read an order to disperse. No-one did; seconds later the police cavalry cantered into sight and sheered through the front row of protesters.

So, without the organisation, it might have ended. Except that people refused to melt away from the police horses and jeer ineffectually from the sidelines. A horse went over, then another, and the Front were led forward so fast that they were quickly straggling. Then suddenly *the sky darkened* (as they say in Latin epic poetry), only this time with clods, rocks, lumps of wood, planks and bricks. All the time the police and the Front had been regrouping and rerouting and while the Left had apparently been mingling ineffectually, groups had been carefully dismantling the rear walls of a number of derelict

'I want an educated movement. Discontent is not enough, though it is natural and inevitable. My belief is that the old order can only be overthrown by force; and for that reason it is all the more necessary that the revolution should not be an ignorant, but an intelligent revolution.'

William Morris

They did not pass: Lewisham, August 1977.

Red Saunders

Syd Shelton

terrace houses facing the Front's route. A pallid white youth from Lambeth SWP with sneakers, torn bomber jacket and pimples sat and chatted amiably to a heavy dread with red, green and gold tam as they broke the lumps into throwable sizes. The result was mayhem.

The Front found it most difficult to dodge this cannonade while upholding the dignity appropriate to a master race inspecting soon-to-be-deported underlings. The NF march was broken in two, their banners seized and burnt; only thanks to considerable police assistance was a re-formed, heavily protected and cowed rump eventually able to continue on its route to Lewisham. When the bedraggled survivors finally reached their meeting hall, the opening speaker, veteran fascist John Tyndall, who proclaims himself to be something of a tough guy, began, 'I think the Third World War has just started out there.'

As for our side, we were frightened and brave and proud and ashamed all at the same time. As the day became more brutal and frightening and the police, furious at their failure, turned to take revenge on the counterdemonstrators, there was one big flash of recognition on the faces in the groups: between dread and socialist, between lesbian separatist and black parent, between *NME* speedfreak and *ASTMS* branch secretary. We were together.

As planned, the counterdemonstrators regrouped at Lewisham Bridge and continued a running battle with the bedraggled NF marchers, making a second attempt to block the fascists' progress down Lewisham High Street. Here a second phase of the battle commenced as the police, bringing out their new riot shields, attempted to attack the counterdemonstrators. They were singularly unsuccessful. At one point, a detachment of twenty-four policemen, shields at the ready, emerged from the Lewisham police station and met head-on a fusillade of bricks and bottles. Barely breaking step, they reversed and retreated back into the station.

Under Lewisham Bridge, a police van driving far too fast sustained a direct hit on its front windscreen, screeched to a halt and turned on its side. Further down the road, a group of black kids found an unmanned police motorcycle and set fire to it. The SWP, concerned to balance when to go on the offensive and when to withdraw in good order, attempted to regroup at the Ladywell BR station by Vicar's Hill, one of the prearranged fall-back points. But such was the mood that Joanna Rollo, an editor of *Socialist Worker* now leading a sizeable contingent, took the call of 'To the station' as an instruction to

Phil McCowan

advance on the Lewisham police station and took 2000 jubilant marchers to the police headquarters.

The mood was justly euphoric. Not only because of the sense of achievement – they didn't pass, not with any dignity anyway, and the police completely lost the absolute control McNee had boasted about – but also because, at last, we were all in it together.

A lot came out of the events at Lewisham. The SWP made the decision to broaden the base of the anti-fascist movement by initiating the Anti-Nazi League. Rock Against Racism, established the previous year, began to organise in earnest. The black community, who had successfully defended their patch, had had a glimpse of a white anti-racist feeling which was much bigger and more militant than the liberal community-relations tea parties might suggest. A lot of ordinary people thought it was a Good Thing that the Little Hitlers had taken a bit of stick. Every little racialist was made smaller. Many people who had reservations about direct action found themselves regretting they had not been there too.

The scheme for an anti-Nazi united front emerged over Sainsbury's white wine in SWP National Secretary Jim Nichol's back garden in Stoke Newington, two weeks before Lewisham.

The title Anti-Nazi League was deliberately chosen to be as broad as possible. It should be open to people who were pro-immigration control but were prepared to demonstrate against the Nazis. It was to be an anti-movement because a pro-movement would waste too much time arguing about rival utopias. And it was to be pitched far wider than the conventional left and anti-racist opinion to include people from pop culture, sport and entertainment respected by the kids the NF were aiming at. The idea was to be kept very secret and carefully sounded out on people who didn't see a copy of *Socialist Worker* from one year to the next.

Nichol went first to the late Douglas Tilbey, Quaker Labour Party member, magistrate and OBE, 'a really nice guy, very principled on the question of race and always had a bit of time for the SWP'. Tilbey thought it was an excellent idea. Then Nichol put the scheme to Tassaduq Ahmed, a middle-of-the-road Bangladeshi who had been in Britain since 1963. Nichol wanted his opinion because of his contacts with East London Bengalis and Tassaduq relayed to him the concern he also felt about the number of factions that existed within

'Babylon is a state of mind, not geography, Remember that. And it is a state of mind that is prevailing on the earth right now.'

Mikey Cambell

the black communities.

The next barometer was Michael Seifert, the lawyer and Communist Party member, because of his links with trade-union bureaucracy people like Ken Gill, George Guy and Alan Sapper – whose blessing was also going to prove essential. Nichol recalls, 'I said, ''Mike, this is only really going to work if it gets the support of the CP and the left TU leaders. What do you think?'' Mike said, ''I think it's a bloody great idea. But I'm sorry, the CP won't, they'll crucify you. So I'll not mention it to anyone.'' '

It cannot even be said that Nichol's own comrades were wild about the idea. He was met with a yes-well-it-sounds-like-a-good-idea-you-go-and-do-something-about-it response. The reaction of the SWP National Committee was generally cold and there was some argument against the project and spoiling suggestions.

Nichol approached Paul Holborow, who had joined the forerunner of the SWP in Dundee in 1969 and since 1974 had been active in East London, and involved in the successful defence of the Lea Bridge Road mosque, the opposition to the NF newspaper sales in Barking and Stratford shopping precincts, the big anti-racist marches in Ilford and Hoxton and the anti-racist protest strike at Ford's, Dagenham. 'I met him in Tina's Café in Cambridge Heath Road,' Nichol recalls, 'and unfolded the scheme. And he thought. And he said, ''Yes, I'll do it and I think we should get Joanna Rollo to be secretary.'' And what he was thinking was there'd be some sort of paper campaign and he's paper chairman and she'd be paper secretary. And so I had to convince him that it was an active campaign, led from the front. Something that called for a public school boy.'

Holborow, who does combine the Charterhouse air of clipped command with the concern for accuracy of an artillery officer, wasn't anxious to leave East London. But he appreciated the challenge that the rout of the NF at Lewisham presented. 'What happened was very clear. Very many more people were prepared to do something about the Nazis than were in our organisation. The phone had been ringing all day in the national office with a very similar message. People were saying, ''I absolutely support your attack on the Nazis. I'd like to give you money but I don't want to have anything to do with the SWP.'' It was as straightforward as that.'

One of his first steps was to attempt to interest Peter Hain, one of the members of the emerging Labour Left who had a record as an organiser and who, if he got involved, wouldn't be content just to be a figurehead. Hain said, as he always does, that he had no time, so Holborow eventually had to meet up with him at Clapham Common and drive with him in his car to his home, managing to catch his interest by Putney and inveigle his way indoors.

Holborow then canvassed Ernie Roberts, the Labour MP, in the Centerprise Bookshop in Hackney. Roberts, an oddly dapper veteran of the Engineering Union, also liked the idea, got straight to work and at the Labour Party Conference collected the signatures of over forty MPs. A founding statement was drawn up which drew attention to the growth of the Nazi groups and proposed a sliding scale of activity aimed to oppose the NF wherever they tried to influence events. This could range from organising public removal of racist graffiti on housing estates, tackling racist bullying and Young National Front leafleting in school playgrounds, and organising occupational, workplace and professional ginger groups, to stopping the NF when they marched, without which all the rest was somewhat pointless.

Holborow was introduced to David King, the *Sunday Times Magazine* tyro, who has created his own distinctive graphic style from a resynthesis of Russian revolutionary idioms. They struck it off well and in the course of a short

Paul Trevor

'Since I come 'ere I never met a single English person who 'ad any colour prejudice. Once, I walked the whole length of a street looking for a room, and everyone told me he or she 'ad no prejudice against coloured people. It was the neighbour who was stupid. If only we could find the ''neighbour'', we could solve the entire problem.'

A. G. Bennett

chat mapped out the graphic style of the ANL, agreeing on the arrow logo and the slogan *Never Again*.

The founding meeting was eventually held in the House of Commons on 9th November 1977 and a steering committee was elected with four Labour MPs, including Neil Kinnock, and the actress Miriam Karlin, the playwright David Edgar, and the economist Nigel Harris. A range of 'names' became sponsors – writers, MPs and academics, footballers, boxing champions and comedians.

The growth of local groups was phenomenal. In view of the especially oppressive but, at this time, surprisingly little-known attacks by the Nazis on feminists, homosexuals and sexual progressives, as well as the overall fascist vision of women in the home and the kitchen endlessly breeding warriors for

Dan Jones

'People can be blinded by their own fears, their solitary weakness. Then they fight each other. They take out the savagery of the system on its victims – in a word, racialism.'
Nigel Harris

the master race, the ANL made specific approaches to the women's movement and the gay movement. And the pioneering and inventive *Teachers Against the Nazis*, who issued their own TANkit teaching aids, were only the first of nearly forty occupational ANL subgroups. Railway workers, miners, engineers, Ford workers, electricians and town-hall workers all had their own badges out within weeks. There were *Aardvarks Against the Nazis*, *Left-Handed Vegetarians Against the Nazis*; patrons of the Manchester pub the Albert minted *Albert Against the Nazis*; a trio of journalists with a shared admiration for malt whisky got a limited edition of three *Drunks Against the Nazis* printed, and so on. In Manchester, Colin Barker thinks 'the ANL took off because of the badges'. Collectors found a complete set required not just a lapel but an overcoat.

The ANL was keen to get a high media profile and an image of activists

rather than do-gooders and so an instant but highly effective protest was sprung on a former Waffen SS officer who was in London, at the home of Tory MP Jonathan Guinness, to promote a book on the SS. Holborow breezed into this press conference waving his new *Never Again* poster and turned the event into an advert for the ANL that hit the ten o'clock TV news.

Another instantaneous protest was organised against the Old Bailey Judge McKinnon, who had presided at the jury trial in November 1977 which found the leader of the British National Party, Kingsley Read, innocent of inciting racial hatred. Kingsley Read had greeted the news of the fatal stabbing of Gurdip Singh Chagger with the war cry 'One down, one million to go'. Judge McKinnon wished him well from the dock, and added, 'Read is obviously a man who has the guts to stand up in public for the things he believes,' and advised the man, 'By all means propagate the views you hold.' And to *The Times* on 8th January 1978 the judge insisted he had 'No regrets. This is a free country. Or was until this act came in. An Englishman should be able to say what he likes.' The ANL call for his dismissal was widely applauded.

Even the predicted tension within the League between liberals and revolutionaries over the question of physical confrontation didn't cause the problems anticipated. As a conventional political operation it was already a considerable success. But it presented an opportunity to do something far bigger, to take the revolutionary cultural spirit of the May Events of 1968 and translate them to the British racial crisis of the late seventies. For what really announced the ANL as a mass movement – a movement which genuinely brought culture and politics into each other's arms and set them dancing – was the alliance with Rock Against Racism in the great Victoria Park outdoor carnival of April 1978.

'Win the energies of intoxication for the revolution.'
Walter Benjamin

Karen, Scruff and other members of the RAR office posse at Victoria Park, Carnival One.

ROCKIN' AGAINST IT

Rock Against Racism, although it addressed the same problems as the ANL, was of different parentage and the elder of the anti-racist twins by eighteen months. There were only three commandments over our baby's fake leopard-skin-lined cot: Vladimir Mayakovsky's admonition, 'The streets are our brushes and the squares our palettes,' Wilhelm Reich's advice, 'Politicise private life, fairs, dance-halls, cinemas, markets, bedrooms, hostels, betting shops! Revolutionary energy lies in everyday life,' and the French students' 1968 barricade cry, 'All power to the imagination!'

In my dream of our christening party Billie Holiday dueted with Paul Robeson, Archie Shepp jammed with Django Reinhart and Max Roach, James Baldwin swapped jokes with Dorothy Parker, and Colin MacInnes served behind the bar. For these people were our cultural godparents. Holiday fought racism with every breath of her body and *Strange Fruit*, her anti-lynching song, was premiered at Café Society (*The Right Place for the Wrong Person*), one of the first clubs in Manhattan to be genuinely racially mixed. Robeson, Negro athlete, actor, singer and Communist, was attacked by American fascists when he sang at an open-air political benefit at Poughkeepsie. Dorothy Parker was a founder member of the original Anti-Nazi League formed in Hollywood in 1934, and Colin MacInnes, along with John Dankworth, Cleo Laine, Max Jones and other British jazz musicians, had set up the Stars' Campaign for Inter-Racial Friendship after the Notting Hill riots in London in 1958. Shepp had said in 1968, 'My alto is like the Viet Cong's machine gun,' Reinhart's gypsy jazz guitar had been banned by the pro-Nazi Vichy government as *'decadent'*, and Max Roach, the dynamo of be-bop, set Martin Luther King's speech 'I have seen a vision' to drums. And Baldwin had stated, 'If the word integration means anything, this is what it means: that we, with love, shall force our brothers to see themselves as they are, to cease fleeing from reality and to begin to change it.'

On one level Rock Against Racism was an orthodox anti-racist campaign simply utilising pop music to kick political slogans into the vernacular. But on another level, it was a jail break. We aimed to rescue the energy of Russian revolutionary art, surrealism and rock and roll from the galleries, the advertising agencies and the record companies and use them again to change reality, as had always been intended. And have a party in the process. RAR's official slogan was *Reggae, Soul, Rock and Roll, Jazz, Funk and Punk: Our Music* but the label sewn inside our zoot suits read *By Courtesy of Constructivism, the Cinema and the Electric Guitar: Our Culture.*

Lady Day, Billie Holiday.

'Instead of telling me what she wanted me to do, she'd get all excited because her husband was waiting, start hollering at me and calling me ''nigger''. I didn't know what it meant. But I could guess from the sound of her voice.'

Billie Holiday

53

'You own the music and we make it.'

Archie Shepp

In his 1977 study of nationalism and social crisis, *The Break-up of Britain*, Tom Nairn looks forward to a 'new progressive and generous cultural movement which will be an alternative to *nationalist* revival and may one day serve as a cultural bond between sectarian Marxism and a wider popular movement.' Nairn predicted exactly what Rock Against Racism became. But RAR's own strength was that it was not a decision of the intellect but came out of the cultural experience of the first generation to have grown up in multi-racial inner-urban Britain. It was a generation who mixed loyalty to the spirit of the Commune, Bolshevism and the German revolutionary Left with post-war, post-electronic modernist culture. So RAR was not started by university graduates but by cultural autodidacts working in photography, the glossies, theatre, rock and roll, graphic design and fashion. When we were finding our way to Marxism in the 1960s our common influences were not only Mayakovsky, El Lissitzky, Tatlin, Brecht, Grosz and Heartfield but surrealism, the cinema, Tamla Motown, the *Village Voice*, Cadillac fins and American pop art. We plagiarised from far wider sources: Hanoi banana labels, Istanbul daily papers, Vivienne Westwood's clothes, Cecil Beaton, the US Air Force, Matisse (for colour), Man Ray, the underground press, Kraus's *Die Fackel*, mid-period Jean-Luc Godard, Situationism, always backed by the music of Jamaica and the American cities.

Red Saunders's experience was one example of the sixties self-education we had all been through in some form or other. He remembers, 'I was just a working photographer and then the art got to me, typography, Rodchenko's posters, Mayakovsky's poetry. I was educated by the theatre group CAST (the Cartoon Archetype Slogan Theatre), it was the rock on

Top to bottom: **Victor Vasarely's 'Black & White'; Charlie Parker; Heartfield's Berlin 1936.** Below: **Youthfuls, John Lennon and Stevie Wonder.**

Andy Dark

Syd Shelton

which everything was based – brilliant minds and high energy – who taught me everything I know, about culture, politics, organising. So that we would be reading Preobrazhensky this week, right, then we're off to see the Prague Theatre of the Black and then it's *The Crimes of M Lange* on at the Kilburn Grange. It trained you for cultural fanaticism. It wasn't just entertainment and you'd go out for a meal afterwards. We'd go back to the flat, eat sardines on toast, get herbed up and analyse it all night.'

Peter Bruno, another CAST actor and a signatory of the letter that founded RAR, remembers seeing Carné's *Les Enfants du Paradis* eight times and dismantling it differently each time. 'What people never remember about the sixties is that it was a period in which, thank God, everyone was prepared to get a bit intellectual about things. It was dead serious.'

I had been brought up to regard Billie Holiday as possessing one of the most expressive and affecting voices in music, my skin has been burnt by the dry ice of James Baldwin's prose, my map of the world turned upside down by *The Black Jacobins*, my pulse set racing by Charlie Parker's assault on the Winter Palace of jazz, tears brought to my boyish eyes by Miriam Makeba singing in the musical *King Kong*, my Marxism shaped by encounters with the views of C. L. R. James and W. E. B. DuBois, and my Dalston Sundays slipstreamed by yearning, sublimely logical dub floating up from underneath the Cortinas. The Black experience is critical to the twentieth century, to modern culture and to me – my pleasure and my understanding.

Tens of thousands of white people with different lists share the same identification. What lent RAR its particular urgency was that it wasn't just fund raising for a good cause out there but we were defending and thereby redefining ourselves and the cultural mix of the inner cities in which we had

'Now I can't deal with poetry as some high-art form existing for the beauty of itself – no, mon, it must enlighten, it must be a means to *emphasise* experience.'
Mutabaruka

Top left: **Falls Road, Belfast.**
Top right: **Aldgate, London.**
Below (r–l): **Vivienne Westwood; Fritz Lang's Metropolis; Malcolm X.**

grown up and in which our children are now finding their feet.

RAR cured the schizophrenia between Marxist politics and modern culture. After the RAR letter, 'There was a tremendous relief,' Red Saunders remembers. 'At last someone had said, be proud of using electric modern music and culture to fight the Nazis and racism, not Hungarian linocuts.'

Roger Huddle remembers: 'The most staggering thing about RAR was that not only did revolutionaries who were my age also happen to have gone down the mod clubs in Wardour Street in the early sixties, but they never even let on that they were also J. B. Lenoir fans and had obscure Delta blues records tucked away in the back of their collections. With RAR, we could all come out.' For Syd Shelton the photographer and designer, it was: 'Like you've come from the working class, you've been a lifelong socialist but you've also secretly loved Jaguar XJ6 saloons. Now RAR suddenly tells you, after the revolution, we're all going to drive XJ6s.'

Black music was our catechism, not just something we listened to in our spare time. It was the culture which woke us up, had shaped us and kept us up all night, blocked in the Wardour Street mod clubs, fanatical on the Thames Valley R & B circuit, queueing all down Gerrard Street to see Roland Kirk in Ronnie Scott's old basement. It was how we worked out our geography, learnt our sexuality, and taught ourselves history. There was no question of slumming or inverted snobbery, we went for black music because it was so strong rhythmically, there was a passion in it, it was about life and had some point to it. And if white musicians were as good and as exciting (as Georgie Fame, Alexis Korner and the early Stones certainly were) we worshipped them too.

Because of Lenin and Marx we had some analysis of the social contradictions which had produced the music. We also knew how white musicians and the record industry had copied, borrowed and stolen from the black origins, from the Original Dixieland Jazz Band through Elvis's songs by Arthur Crudup and Otis Blackwell, Pat Boone's cleaned-up cover of Little Richard's *Tutti Frutti*, Led Zeppelin's Willie Dixon references on *Whole Lotta Love*, right down to Clapton's hapless impersonation of Marley's insurrectionary *I Shot The Sheriff* and the Police's preposterous white reggae. Despite all that, we knew from experience that music – good music – of all popular cultures had the potential to be the best sort of race relations going, as Selwyn Baptiste of the Notting Hill Carnival used to say. In some ways the Soho jazz and blues clubs had been pioneering islands of racial equality since the forties.

Our clubland apprenticeship was, of course, a phase. As Roger Huddle now says, 'R & B's attraction was the passion, which was as strong as one's political feelings. But then the whole world of music opens up to you, not just jazz, but then you can start listening to John Cage, Steve Reich and Schoenberg because you've broken out of the pop trap, you're into the universality of sound.' Other people and other generations are shaped by different passions, fashions and political movements. But our experience had taught us a golden political rule: how people find their pleasure, entertainment and celebration is also how they find their sexual identity, their political courage and their strength to change.

RAR's first major production was held at the Royal College of Art in December 1976, where the chairman of the student union was in the SWP. Red had been approached by two delightful West Indian hustlers who could see the potential of the idea: 'Maaan, you could make a fortune,' they told him, plying him with rum. 'Give us the deal, maan. Just sign here. What car you want?' They took him to see Matumbi in a ram-packed all-black South London blues club. Dennis Bovell, Matumbi's leader, only recently out of prison after a police raid on his sound system, agreed to play the RCA with Carol Grimes,

'In all the regions in which an advanced culture has been found there has been a conquest of one people or peoples by others. The claim that cross-breeds are degenerate is refuted by the actual fact that the whole population of the world is hybrid and becoming increasingly so.
M. S. Ashley-Montague

On the bus to West Runton, Norwich.

Syd Shelton

ROCK AGAINST RACISM

REGGAE
SOUL
ROCK 'N' ROLL
JAZZ FUNK AND P
- OUR MUSIC!

ROYAL COLLEGE OF ART

MATUMBI,

CAROL GRIMES AND
LONDON BOOGIE BAND, LIMOSINE

FRIDAY DEC. 10
8 TILL 2
3 BARS - FOOD

R.C.A. KENSINGTON GORE, ALBERT HALL ENT
£1·20 AT THE DOOR
£1·00 IN ADVANCE FROM S.U. R.
50p SCHOOL LEAVERS, UNEMPL

ROCK AGAINST RACISM

Matumbi.

Red Saunders

Olli Kauniskangas

Syd Shelton

the London Boogie Band and Roger Huddle's immaculate R & B disco, the Night Train.

It was a wonderfully bizarre night with punks in tens, then hundreds. The art schoolies were outdone by the sheer nerve of fifteen-year-old girls with mauve and green hair, string boleros, leotards and plastic flower wedgies. The kids swanned round as if they owned the college. Freaks from past history and costume-drama cases from the summer of love queued up quite amiably with maximum dreadlocks and members of the Clash and the Slits. The music was extremely loud, the dancing very rowdy and the stalls sold political and anti-racist literature, food and banners. Something was in the air: not just dope, but a serious music-politics-black-white mix-up.

Matumbi were heaven: a springy bass line, urgent near-rock lead guitar, horns playing as if backing Otis Redding but lyrics about London betting

Top: **Fans, RAR gig, Southall, November 1977.** Middle: **Joe Strummer and friends share a joke.** Bottom: **Rock and roll revival gig, Royalty pub, Southgate.** Right: **Karen and the touring RAR stall.**

'You receive your newspaper in the morning. You read how comfortable survival has been made for you.'
Karl Kraus

shops and boozers. Matumbi and Carol Grimes were somehow manoeuvred together, the punks leapt on stage completely zonked, and seasoned lefties gasped into their mild and bitters. It was as infectious as German measles and melted all the usual show-off super-cool of the RCA, swamping it with bouncing bodies and bass frequencies.

But it was hard going. People would come up and say 'RAR – that's the anti-Eric Clapton group, isn't it?', the Left thought us too punky and the punks feared they would be eaten alive by Communist cannibals.

At the founding conference at the North London Poly in January 1977 it was clear RAR had pulled together a caboodle of oddballs who were going to work together a lot more imaginatively and explosively than the worthies of the conventional anti-racist platforms. There were musicians, theatre workers, punks and politicos who all recognised RAR as something they agreed with

mixture of creativity

Syd Shelton

Red Saunders

Syd Shelton

Top right: **Sharon Spike, fanzine editor and *TH* writer.** Bottom right: **Tulse Hill Comprehensive boys.** Left: **The founder of Teds Against the Nazis.**

'When you wake up, don't forget to . . .
OPEN YOUR EYES
Then you won't walk about all day bumping into things.'
Dr Smartypants

ROCK AGAINST RACISM

LOVE MUSIC
HATE RACISM

'Only one thing could
have stopped our movement—
if our adversaries had
understood its principles
and from the first day
had smashed with the utmost
brutality,the nucleus of
our new movement'
Hitler 1933.

'Never make a politician
grant you a favour.
They will always want
to control you forever.
It takes a revolution
to make a solution'
Bob Marley

'where you find injustice,
the proper form of politeness is
ATTACK'
T-Bone
Slim

WE ARE MANY,
THEY ARE FEW.

SHAKE YOUR
CHAINS TO EARTH,
LIKE DEW.

and, more importantly, could be part of. And young SWP organisers in Sheffield, Paisley and Birmingham were phoning up Red's Soho studio – activists who weren't just keen but who knew how to organise, could get a decent silk-screen poster printed and flyposted, understood the kind of hall to book and how to make the stage look good.

The music press, with the exceptions of Pete Silverton and Miles, were suspicious and cynical about attempts to *'bring politics'* into their precious world of professional attitudinising. But something was happening inside the music and the culture itself. Other inner-city inhabitants were clambering out of the same cultural car crash – the Clash, Johnny Rotten and thousands like them. All of them were anti-racists from the heart and not afraid to say so. The sound systems were whispering and bumping with mighty dub messages produced in London in an emerging UK style. In 1976 the Notting Hill Gate Carnival had been saturated by uniformed and belligerent policemen. The Clash's *White Riot* was inspired by the courage of the black youth who stood up to them. Soweto was rising, Hull prisoners were on the roof, *Gay News* was on trial for blasphemy and nearly a quarter of a million workers marched through London against the Labour government's IMF-ordered cuts. After three years' political slumber, things were beginning to stir again. When Johnny Rotten told Bill Grundy to **'Fuck off'** on Granada TV in December 1976, the punk mood that had been brewing up in the clubs finally punched through into national notoriety.

Punk was simple to analyse: complete mad anarchy. It was another response to the same social crisis which produced the NF's successes and it could go in any direction. The musicians who were riding it knew just how precarious the thing was: in his first important interview, Joe Strummer of the Clash said 'We are against the NF' because he knew the fascists could have a field day in the nihilism which was punk reality when the music stopped. But the punk musicians and fanzine editors equally loathed the moralism of conventional leftist rhetoric about fascism. Fortunately, so did we.

Yes, punk is violent and sexist, the argument went. It's also subversive and disorientating and highly political and about time too. The people who harp on about the ambiguities and the rip-offs and confusion want a reason to disapprove, want youth to fight the correct battles in the language that we have handed down to them. Punks send up a lot of those categories in an unfooled and honest way. What's happening with the fanzine design and writing DIY clothes and the return of singles and independent record labels is a great wave of new energy just when it seemed everything had run out of steam. Where it ends up, which way it goes, depends in part on what people like us do, whether we can improvise and innovate and break our rules to get through to people. Otherwise the business will take back the initiative, even if it takes a year or two. Wanted: garage politics.

RAR decided to start a propaganda magazine: the chosen name was *Temporary Hoarding*. The original idea was half poster, half illustrated lyrics, with some politics in between. We took the ideas of the underground press with its cheap mass production and extensive use of visuals but purged the hippyism, replaced the conceptual squiggles with the harder edge of the punk fanzines and added our dubbed version of Marxism. A real fluidity between music, style and visuals was beginning to be possible. We used found images and automatic writing in *TH* as an equivalent to the scissors-and-paste aesthetics of the Clash's clothes and first album and the unpredictable, manic mixes that geniuses like Lee Perry were producing.

In an early issue, in a parody of Peter Blake's cover for the *Sergeant Pepper* album which instead used as a backdrop the surging crowd at Soweto, we

TH No. 1

T E M P O R A R Y
H O A R D I N G

ROCK AGAINST RACISM No. 1

20p.

We want rebel music, street music. Music that breaks down people's fear of one another. Crisis music. Now music. Music that knows who the real enemy is. Rock against racism.

LOVE MUSIC
HATE RACISM

ROCK AGAINST RACISM

M. Harrison-Goudie

NON WHITE ENTRANCE

pieced together our influences and inspirations in a rebellious montage where trade-union organisers jostled with romantic poets and Russian revolutionaries stood shoulder to shoulder with Irish republicans. In the crowd Muddy Waters brandished a hammer and sickle, André Breton held aloft a placard that read *Don't mourn, organise*, Johnny Rotten lurched ultra-leftward with Lenin shouting after him, Mao became a woman sprinter, Emma Goldman was trying to get a word in between Arthur Scargill and Peter Tosh while Valerie Solanas stared on and Percy Shelley sighed.

Inspired by the post-electronic renaissance that was exploding all around us, with new bands popping up every week, we tried to develop a new visual language. We not only organised the best-dressed gigs in town but photographed them and rearranged that through design and production sessions, working nonstop at weekends in the *Socialist Worker* artroom, sustained by speed and Brick Lane *sag ghost*. We had access, by courtesy of the SWP, to weekend use of a £3000 process camera and a Goss offset litho press the size of five bulldozers.

Ruth Gregory, the painter and graphic designer who was to become editor and the *force tranquille* behind the graphic power of *Temporary Hoarding*, says:

> **Until *TH* the** socialist papers I'd designed were always uphill, always in adversity. Suddenly we had connected, captured the spirit. We were going to change the face of culture as we knew it. Of course it was way over the top. But that was one of its strengths.

Above all *TH* was political with gusto; not afraid to get Andy Dark to photomontage Bowie onto Powell onto Hitler and caption it with Shelley and Malcolm X, to discuss sexual politics in a way that was impossible in gigs, to report regularly on Britain's last colony, Northern Ireland, and to insist that our little Hitlers had their big brothers in power in South Africa. And, as the critic Guy Brett spotted in selecting it for an international collection of *the art of political resistance*, *TH* was 'a brilliant agitator in the campaign against racism and fascism in Britain and against the National Front's efforts to mobilise youth support'.

TH wasn't just an art object but contained information, lots of music, political comment and the practical experience of organising against the NF in a format which never quite made clear where one stopped and the next started. By 1979, *TH* was selling 12,000 copies.

Montage: Roger Huddle, *TH* No. 2

"Career Opportunities
the ones that never knock
Every job they offer you is to keep you out the dock
Career Opportunities.
They offered me the office
They offered me the shop
They said I'd better take anything they'd got
Do you wanna make tea at the BBC?"
"Do you wanna be a cop?"
"I hate the army
an' I hate the RAF

RAR's next concert wasn't put on till 1st May 1977, the first May Day to be an official public holiday in Britain. Red was the producer: 'For the first time I instigated Full Propaganda' which meant pulling out all the theatrical, visual and emotional stops. Advertised on the bill were the young reggae lions Aswad, hard-core punks the Adverts with TV Smith, the African cultural group Steel and Skin, the last incarnation of the Kartoon Klowns, and a host of guests. In the foyer of London's Roundhouse theatre, richly embroidered and lavishly ornamented trade-union banners direct from the May Day parades piled up. Inside, the photographer Gered Mankowitz, who covered the Stones' first tour of America and did their early album covers, was slicing the

Red Saunders

Below: **Members of Handworth's Steel Pulse ponder the Roundhouse stage.** Right: **Kartoon Klowns agitpropping.**

AT THE ROUND HOUSE

MAY 1st

MAYDAY

ROCK AGAINST RACISM

CAROL GRIMES
THE LONDON BOO
AND PAUL JONES
ASWAD STEEL & SKIN
GENERATION X KART

5·00 PM-10·30 PM
Round House, Chalk Farm
Tickets at the door £1/50
with dole card Ba

stage with raking, searing prussic and lemon rock-and-roll lighting.

Robert Galvin, a young art student, had devised an RAR typeface for mass production of banners by which a template alphabet was stencilled onto the self-adhesive plastic fabric Fablon, cut out and stuck down on day-glo cloth from the specialist shops in Berwick Street. So the Roundhouse, melting pot of countercultural sixties, was riotously decorated with colossal red and green, purple and gold, and black and white banners with RAR slogans. On stage members of Aswad, the Adverts, the Carol Grimes band, Ari Up and Tessa from the Slits-to-be and Mitch Mitchell of the Jimi Hendrix Experience-that-was ended the evening with a jam which began slowly (jamming is very much a jazz tradition and, in general, pop musicians loathe it) but built to a tremendous surge of energy between stage and audience as punk icono-clasm, reggae rhythms, blue soul and good ol' rock and roll managed to merge for a common purpose. Paul Jones, a veteran of the R & B days, sang

'I lifted my hat from my face and said in patois – moi veeway – I have arrived. I felt as if I had already won.'

Phyllis Allfrey

63

Red Saunders

**Carol Grimes at the
Roundhouse.**

his heart out and, in one of those moving backstage moments, presented the young drummer of Aswad with a giant spliff and his mouth harp. Carol Grimes summed up the Roundhouse gig: 'It showed that music can break down the barriers. What you want is the jam on stage to be reflected in the audience – it can't be the property of the musicians.'

Then came the Lewisham march. Seven days later, on 21st August, RAR was still high for a joint gig with the Right to Work campaign at Hackney Town Hall. It was packed with post-Lewisham punk pride. Generation X and the Cimarrons were using the mayor's chamber as a dressing room. Along the corridor were the portraits of outstanding leaders of Hackney labour. The two women on the bar were just about concealing their horror at the waves of punks drinking them dry. The lights were useless, the stage was an island, the atmosphere exceptional, everywhere there were faces from New Cross. *Security* was ten of the largest SWP locals with linked arms between band and pogo front line.

Generation X were surprisingly good, especially on John Lennon's *Gimme Some Truth*: the real passion in Billy Idol's voice and Tony James's guitar. The Cims moved straight into their Philadelphia-originated *Ship Ahoy* sequence and it was another world aesthetically, candid, artful, rich in musicianship. Then a momentous jam started with *Gloria*, went into Bob Marley's *Johnny Too Bad* and ended with a gaunt white Generation X hand clamped with a black Cimarrons hand held aloft while everyone in the hall chanted 'Black and white, Black and white'. We felt so strong and so close we didn't need to add *unite*. Billy Idol called it 'One of the greatest nights in my life' and the Cimarrons were moved to record a 12-inch tribute called simply 'Rock Against Racism'.

Meanwhile in the *New Musical Express*, Tony Parsons and Julie Burchill, who had been in the front line of the police-horse charge in New Cross Road, blazed away in the best report written of the Lewisham battle:

> **It's time for** backing up the words with action. This late in the day, too few people are carrying the weight of responsibility for all of us. But perhaps you think this wasn't your battle. Tell it to the blacks. Tell it to the SWP. Tell it to Rock Against Racism. Tell it to Charles Shaar Murray. Tell it to the three thousand. Tell it to the kid who lost his right eye.

'What meaning would there be in bringing down Hitler's system in order to stabilise something which is far bigger and in its different way just as bad?'

George Orwell

Although we argued with them about their kindergarten gestures – the dedication of their tract *The Boy Looked at Johnny* to Menachem Begin, the Stalin and glam-rock fixation – they were solid as rock on racism and, with editor Neil Spencer's invaluable backing, wilted swastikas each week with the sheer venom of their spiky-topped prose in the *NME*. And, extraordinarily, we got the seal of approval from the supercynical Sex Pistols.

I have never been able to understand what is revolutionary in Malcolm McLaren's philosophy, which seems, like a rock-and-roll equivalent of Maynard Keynes, to consist of giving capitalists a *'radical'* rationale for what they ought to do in their own interest anyway. This is, in the record business, to steal musical ideas cheap and sell them expensive. But Sophie Richmond who seemed to do most of the work in the Pistols' management, the Glitterbest Organisation, took a fancy to *Temporary Hoarding* and encouraged RAR to go and interview Johnny Rotten, who was refusing to talk to any of the establishment press. They had, quite wrongly, linked the band with the NF and sensationally misreported the knife attacks that Rotten and Paul Cook had sustained from *'patriots'*, actually NF hit squads.

TEmPORARY HOARDING

No 6 – Summer '78   20p

SKINS
Deptford
Peter
Tosh
Jimmy
Pursey.
Africa
Patrik
Fitzgerald
Adam
+ the ants.

'Moa Anbessa-ah-ah-ah. Got a woman want fe hold little rub, check out Shaka fe play some dubs, check out Fatman fe spin some dubs, Coxone see you come tonight but no bother broke no fight . . .'

Cimarrons

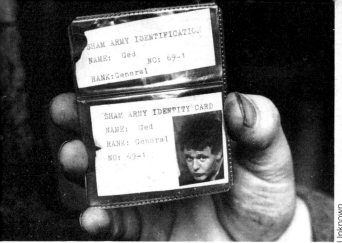

Unknown

Syd Shelton

Top left: **The Sham Army membership card.** Top centre: **RAR security person, Leeds.** Top right. **Vicious slips out of focus.**

Red Saunders

Above: **Kate's RAR supply store.** Below: **Johnny Rotten.**

TH No. 2

The punks had brilliantly panicked the Establishment as well as freaking the Nazis out completely. Instead of a soporific Pimm's Cup summer celebrating the Silver Jubilee, all the royalist trappings, the Ascot hats, reverential BBC commentaries and bunting looked suddenly shabby. *God Save The Queen* went to No. 1 in the hit parade and sent the whole consumptive business up in the best traditions of scurrilous London anti-royalism.

Rotten only pretended to be a yob; his real outlook was Yeatsian. He was a quick-witted Irish-Catholic romantic, but already surrounded by sycophants and with definite signs of rock-and-roll damage. He was also, although it was disguised, very good-looking. And excellent on the NF.

'I despise them. No one should have the right to tell anyone they can't live here because of the colour of their skin or their religion or whatever, the size of their nose. How could anyone vote for something so ridiculously inhumane?'

We got into disagreements about politics, though: he didn't really believe a word of the sub-situationism of McLaren, Julien Temple and crew either, but he'd got a streak of Catholic anti-Communism which, when added to the celebrity he now was lumbered with, threatened to turn him into another ex-working-class rock elitist. But he had certainly not yet become one in 1977. Towards the end of the interview, a Scottish trade unionist from the Right to Work campaign, whose office was over the road, joined in. Rotten and he got on fine, like two old proletarian foot soldiers. Which, in a way, they were. The Scot had seen towns done up so the Queen could pass – 'and the backs, they are like middens'.

We had a lovely time laying out the interview for *TH*. Rotten was such a handsome boy, we decided to drop some pink tone on his teeth to send him up. In real life his front teeth were daffodil with caries. I gave Rotten a prescription for an antibiotic before setting off back to the surgery in Bethnal Green on the 253 bus. But I didn't fancy his chances of cashing it, chemists didn't much care for punks in the summer of 1977. Sure enough, the police were called.

In fact it drizzled incessantly on the Jubilee Day street parties that July. Fireworks were fireworks and there were royalist special effects, but the show was made unbearable by the Home Counties audience, all leather-elbowed sports jackets and talk of being *'in Town'*. London was occupied territory as the unashamedly bourgeois jammed Blackfriars Bridge. All jeered at a bus when it halfway across halted in a jam and blocked their view. 'Be careful, Daddy, he might go on strike,' said Toffeenose Jr. The loyal geography-master type next to me clamped aromatic tobacco into his loyal pipe and sighed. Sighed for the Lost World of the loyal, humble workers, decent bourgeoisie, caring and stylish aristocrats. Humbug. TV-show moppets sang a nonsense

Syd Shelton

Bernie Willcox

jingle about serenity, splendour and loyalty.

Tom Robinson was a lot more straightforward to deal with. He had approached us announcing that he was a gay, anti-racist songwriter who wanted to help. We illustrated his song which succinctly anticipated life under Mrs T., *Winter Of '79*, in *TH* with torn photos from Northern Ireland and put on a joint benefit for Gay Icebreakers and RAR at the North London Poly.

More than anyone, Tom brought sexual politics into RAR. He was out, had worked on the telephone front line of Gay Switchboard and been influenced by the most radical of the New York transvestite groups, Hot Peaches, who had played in London and Bradford in 1976. The Tom Robinson Band was a fairly conventional all-male guitar band with a recognisable enough sound to make one of the first punk Top Ten entries with almost a classic Radio Wonderful hit, *2,4,6,8, Motorway*. Yet Tom utilised this format in songs whose words were almost rearranged news headlines, used performance to communicate political ideas rather than rebel stances, distributed the band's own political fanzine at concerts, and even used the first LP sleeve to advertise political campaigns. But in some weird way Tom's relative political clarity and artistic maturity (his stage act used irony, rhetoric, theatre, music hall as well as rock-and-roll idioms) was held against him by music-press morons who thought you had to be incoherent to make sense.

But although Tom recognised long before Bob Geldof that 'it's frightening, the kind of power and influence something as silly as a rock-and-roll band can wield', that insight alone couldn't close the chasm which loomed between what being a rock star entailed and how a socialist sexual radical would want to live. Still, as TRB rocketed from pub back rooms to *Top of the Pops*, there was none of the big-time 'no time', 'speak to the manager' or 'oops, we seem to have double-booked' which afflicted other RAR-supporting bands when their careers took off. Tom took the RAR star everywhere, on tour and on TV, helped with our office, fitted RAR into tour schedules and loaned us money. And even when he was attacked in Bradford on stage by a 'lesbian zap squad' for singing a pro-women song and the first ever Rock Against Sexism banner was torn down by right-onner-than-thou women, he simply commented, 'That's OK, just hope they do the same to the Stranglers.' Which they didn't. He had to become a diplomat for the Left and was then denounced by it for the crime of being diplomatic. And some nights, when a bitter edge entered his voice as the audience bawled along with *Glad To Be Gay*, he revealed the strain he was under, the vulnerability below the calculated stage presentation and the cost artistry such as his extracted.

Top left: **RAR organiser.** Top centre: **Dennis Bovell's son seen in Shoreditch.** Top right: **Bury RAR gig.**

'Negro and white spirituals share the same Biblical symbolism, but on examining the most extensive collections of white spirituals we have yet to find *any* songs with the explicit sorrow over the actual woes of this world, with the explicit anger against oppression, and with the ringing cries for freedom to be discovered in the Negro songs.'

Alan Lomax

67

TROOPS OUT OF IRELAND

WOULD YOU WANT ONE IN YOUR GARDEN?

'Taking shorthand on a train
at full speed is a really
heroic task.'

Leon Trotsky

68

Within a year punk went from the Roxy to the High Street. Reviled, mocked and censored, it was winning the battle for teenage minds. 'Punk meant no more bullshit,' said Kosmo Vinyl, Ian Dury's aide-de-camp and then Clash minder, 'and we were heard around the world.' The attempted *Anarchy in the UK* tour in December 1976 (the Clash, the Sex Pistols, the Damned, and Johnny Thunders's Heartbreakers) had been brought to a swift standstill by county-council moralists and scandalised record companies. And when it played, it was amateurish and off beam. In Leeds, the local lefties were still at the 'punk, isn't that rather neo-fascist?' stage, the students had Gandalf's Garden tresses, and when the local fascists did beat up a *Socialist Worker* seller in the Poly toilets while the Pistols were on, no one on stage knew about it. Joe Strummer of the Clash was angry and tense. 'We've been on the road five days and this is the first time we get to play.' But in the Leeds Poly urinal was a gay farm worker with a South Yorkshire accent you could hang your coat on who had nothing but black tights and a T-shirt of safety pins underneath his greatcoat.

When, a week after RAR's 1977 May Day Roundhouse show, the Clash's *White Riot* tour hit the Rainbow supported by the Jam (with their Union Jack), the Buzzcocks, and a roots-reggae sound system featuring I Roy and dub from the Revolutionaries, punk was clearly a mass movement. The gaunt Gaumont-Egyptian Rainbow (the old Finsbury Park Astoria which used to house the Beatles' Christmas shows) was filled with marble fountains, scrunched beer beakers and working-class kids in urban destructo chic: Jackson Pollock boiler suits, school-prefect blazers, El Fatah headscarves, blanket pins, aviator goggles, gas masks, studded dog collars, suspender belts and Pacamacs.

Watching couples hobbling up from Finsbury Park tube, it was clear why bondage garments had become an image of liberation. It was better to make explicit the way we are restricted and fetishised than pretend, as the hippies

Caroline Coon

Members of the Clash, Rich Kids and Steel Pulse protest outside the NF HQ, March 1978.

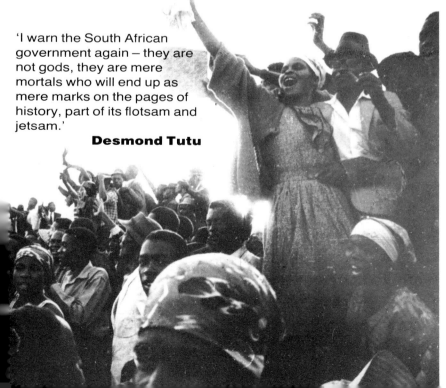

'I warn the South African government again – they are not gods, they are mere mortals who will end up as mere marks on the pages of history, part of its flotsam and jetsam.'

Desmond Tutu

Soweto.

had, to be free. In anti-hippy polemics in *OZ* magazine I had argued in 1967 the acid generation's **'adoption of oriental plumage and religious bric-a-brac is not an answer to the plunder of Indian and African civilisations by imperialism, just impotence and guilt decked out as romanticism'**. But, in opposition, I had offered a puritan working-class world of **'productivity deals, trades councils, football fighting, women talking in launderettes and Guinness'**. Against stylistic revolt was just styleless intransigence. Perhaps the punks were the answer to that dichotomy: subverters of pulp journalism, gutter TV and brutal policemen, who under their monochrome exteriors were peacocks of proletarian revolt.

The Clash hit the stage with a billboard-size photo blow-up of British coppers under attack at the Notting Hill street festival the previous August, and went straight into *White Riot*, a cleverer lyric than the title suggested. Without warning, they had become rock stars, with Mick Jones posturing round the stage like an old-fashioned guitar hero. Strummer had kept his head and announced their wailing punk reworking of Junior Murvin's dreamy *Police And Thieves* like this: **'Last week 119,000 people voted National Front in London. Well, this next one's by a wog. And if you don't like wogs, you know where the bog is.'** The bog was in a very wretched state and being used enthusiastically for all sorts of purposes by both sexes, in an excess of new-wave iconoclasm.

We wanted to connect up the punk explosion with the anti-racists and the rank-and-file trade unionists, who, unlike their union chiefs, were prepared to make a fight over rising unemployment. We also subscribed to the first maxim of surrealism, that to create the most powerful impact you bring together two things as far removed as possible.

So, in the late summer of 1977, RAR organised joint Right to Work and Rock Against Racism gigs on the route through northeast England taken by the Right to Work marchers on their way to the Blackpool Trade Union Congress. We were given half-promises by the Glitterbest office that the Sex Pistols would play at our Wigan Casino gig. In the spirit of the times RAR advertised *Special Mystery Guest* and, on 3rd September 1977, found that 2000 Lancashire punks had Wigan under siege. It was the usual Roxy montage but with the added ingredient of sheer Northern brass neck and friendliness. Girls in matching corsets, suspenders, plastic macs and stilettos strode about arm in arm, a send-up of *Reveille*'s fantasies. Ripped and torn UB40s greeted each other with horrific leers, cuffs and thumps of courteous mock violence. The Right to Work marchers on their way to the TUC at Blackpool leapt about in fluorescent orange jackets with punk song titles Pentelled over them and slogans like *I riot in the presence of fascists*. It was enough to give Len Murray a heart attack.

If the Pistols meant what they sang, they should have been there that night . . . but they weren't. As the night went on, our fate seemed uncertain. Would we be torn apart by disgruntled mobs or just drowned in gob? The entire ornate building shuddered as everyone pogoed on to Sex Pistol records chanting **'No future, no future'** long after the record had finished. But no one did riot and, in a way, it was good to use the Sex Pistols as a metaphor rather than as a band. **'Well, they was 'ere in spirit,'** said a philosophical Barnsley punk as we shiftily took down the Fablon Day-Glo banners.

The *Temporary Hoarding* of December 1977 had interviews with the Tom Robinson Band and Poly Styrene, Bobby Campbell, the Communist Party sports journalist, on Wolf Bierman and dissident East European rock (**'Don't be a no-hoper. Confirm'**), and Lucy Toothpaste on sexual politics (**'If there's**

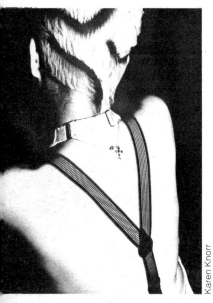

Karen Knorr

one thing that upsets a master race as much as a blatant black, it's a blatant gay'). It also had a new tone of confidence.

RAR is a year and a bit old. We've managed to survive. We've raised the slogan at over 200 gigs. We've sold about 12,000 badges (1000 in Sweden). We've got out four *Temporary Hoardings*. We want more people to write to us to tell us what's happening around them. We want *TH* to survive. Get up, stand up – fight for what is right.

international

To the punks, Red said, 'You can shout arsehole as long as you want but if the authorities stop you from playing and generally hinder your rights, the only way to fight back is to get organised.' And to the Rastas, Benji Arambi, a Waltham-

The Ruts' bass player flat out on stage.

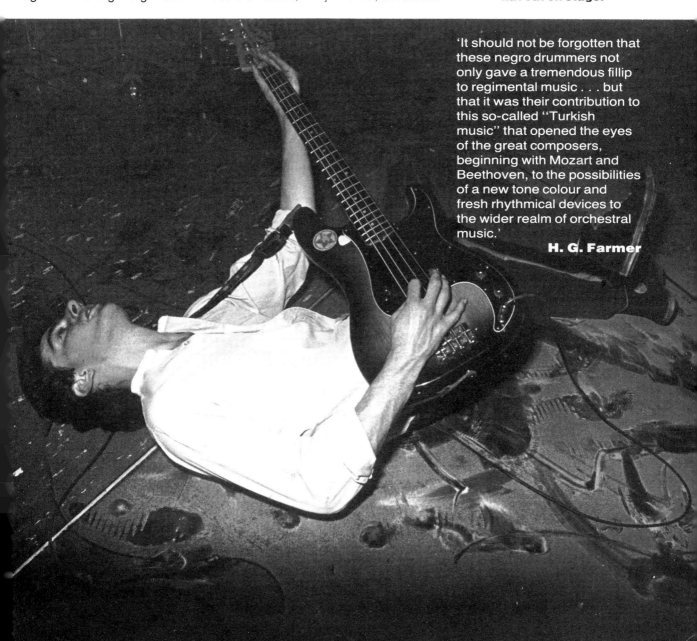

'It should not be forgotten that these negro drummers not only gave a tremendous fillip to regimental music . . . but that it was their contribution to this so-called "Turkish music" that opened the eyes of the great composers, beginning with Mozart and Beethoven, to the possibilities of a new tone colour and fresh rhythmical devices to the wider realm of orchestral music.'

H. G. Farmer

stow DJ, advised: 'The time has come when I and I children of Jah Rastafari got to realise socialism is a bit of groundation – a movement for us.'

RAR was a going concern and about the only *'political'* thing viewed with any respect by musicians made habitually cynical by the excesses of their industry. Bands were increasingly approaching RAR, volunteering to gig. Our horizons dilated. We tried to evolve a division of labour within RAR in which everyone did their creative best and people were powered by pride and enjoyment rather than a feeling someone was giving us marks out of ten for commitment. Still more importantly, local RAR groups sprouted up, inspired by do-it-yourself punk ethic and a determination to get the message heard. There were RAR groups in Leeds and Birmingham and Glasgow and Deptford mixing musicians, artists, designers and socialists, putting on gigs

'In the present state of society, happiness is only possible to artists and thieves.'
Oscar Wilde

Above: **Soweto.** Below: **Misty on stage during the Militant Entertainment tour.**

Syd Shelton

72

and starting up bands. RAR was helping to fuel a second wave of punk which was producing regional outcropping of bands like the Mekons and the Gang of Four from Leeds, the Au Pairs, UB40 and the Beat from Birmingham, and, most wonderful of all, the Two-Tone label, the Midlands' short-winded Tamla-Motown.

And for every International Marxist Group member with a pink rinse who wanted Joe Strummer's home phone number, there were ten young bands who supported our slogans and whom RAR could help to an audience. Indeed, 1977 ended with another remarkable gig at the Royal College of Art, produced entirely without help from RAR headquarters. John *'I do video'* Dennis, who became a full-time worker for RAR in 1978, and Wayne Minter, students at the college, put together a bill of 999, the staccato punk band; Misty, the roots rockers from the West London railway town of Southall, who

'Truth is a diamond
A diamond is hard
You don't exist
Without your Barclaycard.'
Adrian Mitchell

Below: **999 fans and vocalist, Royal College of Art.**

Red Saunders

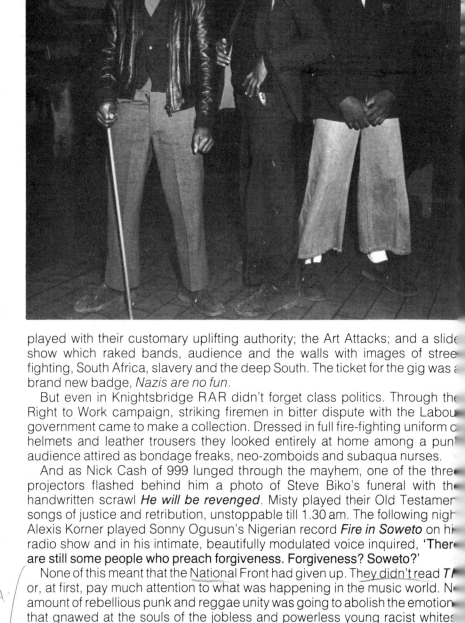

Top left: **RAR's first video.** Top right: **Moss Side militant sounds.** Above: **Striking firemen collect from punks at the RCA.**

Anti-Front demonstrators in Leicester.

played with their customary uplifting authority; the Art Attacks; and a slide show which raked bands, audience and the walls with images of street fighting, South Africa, slavery and the deep South. The ticket for the gig was a brand new badge, *Nazis are no fun*.

But even in Knightsbridge RAR didn't forget class politics. Through the Right to Work campaign, striking firemen in bitter dispute with the Labour government came to make a collection. Dressed in full fire-fighting uniform of helmets and leather trousers they looked entirely at home among a punk audience attired as bondage freaks, neo-zomboids and subaqua nurses.

And as Nick Cash of 999 lunged through the mayhem, one of the three projectors flashed behind him a photo of Steve Biko's funeral with the handwritten scrawl *He will be revenged*. Misty played their Old Testament songs of justice and retribution, unstoppable till 1.30 am. The following night Alexis Korner played Sonny Ogusun's Nigerian record *Fire in Soweto* on his radio show and in his intimate, beautifully modulated voice inquired, 'There are still some people who preach forgiveness. Forgiveness? Soweto?'

None of this meant that the National Front had given up. They didn't read *TI* or, at first, pay much attention to what was happening in the music world. No amount of rebellious punk and reggae unity was going to abolish the emotion that gnawed at the souls of the jobless and powerless young racist whites. Indeed, exactly the same feelings – of desire to shock, of mental oppression of anger at official smugness – which were utilised so creatively in punk rock's emancipating outburst, were exploited in a reactionary, destructive and generally brainless way by the opportunity the Front provided to, as Ken Leach, the anti-fascist vicar of St Matthews, Bethnal Green, put it, 'expand vandalism into a political movement'.

BREWING IT UP

RACISM IS AS British as Biggles and baked beans. You grow up with it: the golliwogs in the jam, *The Black and White Minstrel Show* on the TV and CSE History at school. It's about Jubilee mugs and Rule Britannia and how we singlehandedly saved the ungrateful world in the Second War. Gravestones, bayonets, forced starvation and the destruction of the culture of India and Africa were regrettable of course, but without our Empire the world's inhabitants would still be rolling naked in the mud, wouldn't they? However lousy our football teams or run-down our Health Service, we have the private compensation that we are white, British and used to rule the

'The British don't stand on the doorstep gossiping, or form a crowd on the pavement to talk about the latest ballad. I notice some West Indians still have that habit and I can tell you it isn't one that English people like. What they like is politeness.'
Going to Britain? — a BBC guide to West Indian immigrants

John Sturrock (Network)

Unknown

waves. It would be pathetic if it hadn't killed and injured and brutalised so many lives. Most of the time British racialism is veiled behind forced smiles, charming policemen and considerate charities. But when times get hard, the newest arrival is the first to be blamed. Once they kicked in Protestant French settlers, then tormented the Irish construction workers who built our roads and railways. From the 1880s to 1939 it was the Jews, refugees from unspeakable brutality in Eastern Europe, who became victims and scapegoats once again in London and Leeds.

ONCE AGAIN RACIALISM is defeated by ordinary people's solidarity, eminent people say it will never happen again, until, lo and behold, times get bad and jobs are hard to find and wages are washed out and life gets lousy. And then the junk images of racialism, the debris of 500 years surges up again and the Beast begins to stir. They need a racial problem to distract people from the real ones. They need an answer for people who don't want to think. In 1977 the answer is: blame the blacks.

LAST YEAR IN Britain saw racial violence worse than the height of Mosley's anti-Jew campaign

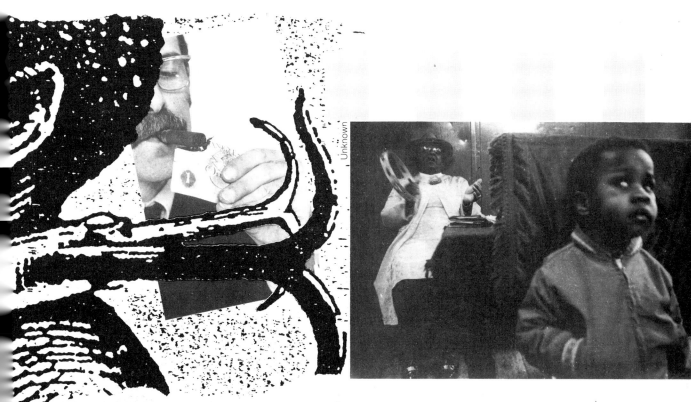

Unknown

'At the birth of the Union of South Africa, Calvin and Darwin shook hands over the chained body of the black.'
Ken Jordaan

in the Thirties. Gurdip Chagger, Dinesh Choudry and Ribbi Al Hadid were stabbed to death in racial murders. Dozens of blacks have been injured by racialists, egged on every morning by the *Mail* and *Express* who made their acts of hatred respectable. Fascists, their spiked Union Jacks and slow military drums under heavy police protection, forced their unwelcome way through Hackney, Bradford, Leicester. Repatriation, which means forced deportation, which means hunting down and rounding up blacks, is informally supported by the Tory Party. And the Labour Party has no answer, except to cringe.

FROM THE WIRE **cages in Heathrow Airport's immigrant compounds to the gleaming Alien Registration computer in Holborn, a new colour bar stretches. Every retreat by officialdom inflames the appetite of the Right. Once again racialism is back. It is growing where it is not challenged. And challenged it must be. For when racialists rule, millions die.**

From *Temporary Hoarding*, Issue 1, September 1977

THE REAL GANGSTERS COME

The NF were after the skinheads and, via them, the punks. Skin bravado was, in fact, loser nihilism; all they were good at was aggro and kicking people when they were down. Their power came from having nothing to lose. They knew where they were (lost) and what they were (rubbish) in a world which didn't even need their muscle power any more. So to deal with them you had to be as efficiently violent as they, but simultaneously unimpressed with the macho nonsense, and you had to take the piss out of their elaborate male self-hatred. RAR needed a difficult mix of heavyweight security and relaxed, seductive rhythms. The skins' Achilles heel was that being deliberately ugly and invulnerable was not fun. The aggro had little style, the clothes had no colour, the dances had no sexuality, the exuberance lay only in hitting or being hit. Sham, Madness, the Angelic Upstarts, and all the bands to which the fascist skins desperately tried to adhere, quickly dissociated themselves. Not out of liberal sentiment or record-company pressure but because the bands just weren't racist or violent (musicians seldom are) and the skin leftovers were little else.

The Upstarts were from the Newcastle-on-Tyne dock area and their leader Mensi was a headbanging socialist who had come into contact with the Left during the campaign over Liddle Towers's death in police custody in February 1976. Madness were Camden Town ska freaks whose first single was an *énervé* cover of a Prince Buster classic. But when they played the Market

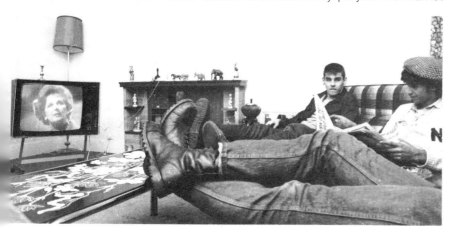

Poster: Edinburgh RAR

THE REAL GANGSTERS COME

ANGELIC
upstarts
metropa
D†S BAND
AND T.H.E.S.P.
SPG

Tavern in Chapel Market it was carpeted with Islington fascists looking to latch on to the band. Madness were going to have to get to grips with at least one leading member of their entourage and tell some of their following they weren't wanted. But the band had the intelligence to do just that, and went on to be one of the most creative and consistent survivors of the era.

When the full honour guard of the British Movement, a paramilitary fascist group, seized the stage at a Sham 69 Rainbow gig and stood there seventy strong *Sieg Heil*-ing, RAR decided the only reply was to put Sham 69 on with a reggae band in central London. But by February 1978, the date of our gig, Sham's last three London venues had been trashed. Two thousand pounds' worth of damage had been done at the London School of Economics, including an espresso machine lobbed out of a second-floor window. The Roundhouse had been tyrannised by running squads of skins. The college admin at Central Poly were apprehensive. But RAR went ahead promoting the gig as *Smash Race Hate in '78*. There were private misgivings that it could instead turn out to be us who got smashed. There was strong pressure from Polydor, Sham's recording company, to cancel. But if RAR meant anything, it meant preaching to the unconverted.

Jimmy Pursey, Sham's vocalist and leader, was OK: a lot of mouth, as desperate to be a star as Judy Garland, but basically a greyhound fancier from Hersham. He couldn't sing but he was a great performer. He was torn between what he knew was right and his racist friends who ran the sound crew and security. The first step was to ease him off the fence.

Jimmy and Misty, the Southall Rastas, got together before the gig and reasoned together. Jim made a clear statement: '**I believe that black and white must live together. We make this stand at this gig to say that.**' Dave Parsons, Sham's guitarist, stated, '**When I look at people it's not colour but people I see.**'

Muscle was provided by the *'fives'* from the docks and North London who had been so effective at Lewisham. Benji Arambi's Unity Hi-Fi Sound System from Dagenham was guarded by his box boys and Misty brought some Southall youth. But there was no real way we could pick out the British Movement from the ordinary skinheads. Anyway, the thing was not about punishment or paranoia but to show that RAR could hold the gig, support Jimmy and ease the fans in the right anti-racist direction, if necessary separating them by force. Fire whistles were distributed to our stewards. The systematic frisking for weapons on the door was done by women. But the college was a sieve and we couldn't hold all entrances. Backstage was a joke; Sham's British Movement mates had taken over and had invited in half of Millwall. Misty just ignored them and sat calmly smoking ganja and smacking down dominoes in the middle of what was left of the dressing room. They were surrounded by about twelve six-foot skins, crombies oozing menace, little tin Union Jack badges glinting from the lapels.

After three hours of high tension, our stewards were starting to crack, coming up with new sightings of known BMers and promises of bundles which would make Altamont look like tea and cucumber sandwiches. Paranoia richocheted around. The black kids were tooled up, so were the dockers in our security team. Mary Larner from the SWP print shop had a ruck with a skin kid: '**I 'ate coons,**' he said. '**I've got a black bloke and a black kid,**' Mary snapped back, '**and I'll have you for mutton if you lay a hand on either of them.**' Mary was a cockney too and old enough to be his mother. The kid backed off; his friends were shamed, little boys again.

Sham went on. Several charges were made at the stage by the fascists but they were tastefully eased back. '**If this gaff blows, it won't end till someone's dead,**' said Eddie Prevost from the Royal Group of Docks Shop Stewards

Nina, Patsy, Robert and anti-racist Danish pastries.

Red Saunders

Top: **Jimmy's greyhounds.**
Above: **Jimmy Pursey on mike.**

Top: **Sikh rockers.** Right: **Benji Arambee's Walthamstow record shop.**

between songs. '**I prefer love and peace myself,**' he added reflectively.

Suddenly Misty and Jim '*Sham*' Pursey with a Rasta tam were on stage together, singing the old skin moonstomp classic *The Israelites*. The concert was over, without blood. The three coachloads of police who had been parked two streets away all night rolled away quietly on the wet roads.

Jimmy Pursey, terrified on the night, was in his element afterwards. 'It made my day. Because I said it was the last time I'd play London if there was any trouble. A lot hung on me, you know. We was the ones who was sacrificing ourselves by making that statement and we proved a point.'

'Them didn't look the kind of
  police me could give a fiver
First thing that come into me
  head:
Good thing me hide my
  ganja!'

Smiley Culture

It had been a grim evening, but it had worked. The jazz critic Brian Case wrote it all up for *NME* the next week with customary insouciance.

Actually, since the rachets of the Immigration Act are already as tight as they can go, the only possible depopulative move would be forced repatriation and since emigration has exceeded immigration since the Second World War, this would seem loopy. Have the newcomers destroyed the British way of life? Well, I don't know that I'd hold them answerable for the demise of the brown penny, feet 'n' inches, the sovereignty of Westminster, the leafy lane, the healthy rabbit and the rentable value of Centre Point and I'm

plumb certain I don't want my head sent back to Ireland and my ass to Wales.

'Now my man, don't want you to worry about one thing. What we's gonna give you ain't gonna be nothing but them solid, old, real-gone, red beans and rice-ly kind of music, kind ever'body can shake a leg to. Yes, suh, we aims to please.'

Charlie Parker

The Anti-Nazi League, founded a year after RAR but usually, on the grounds of greater respectability, regarded as the parent organisation, was anxious to hold a joint demonstration with RAR. Although none of the London local councils would help, the GLC gave us permission to use Victoria Park, the 290-acre *East End Hyde Park* which had been the rallying spot of London Chartists in 1848. The date decided was 30th April 1978.

There was obvious unity of purpose between RAR and the ANL, but also creative tension: we were approaching the same problem from opposite directions. We agreed on the format: a juxtaposition of a political meeting in Trafalgar Square and an open-air concert in Victoria Park would make the politics more fun and the music more political. But RAR's unannounced ambition was to turn the event into the biggest piece of revolutionary street theatre London had ever seen, a tenth anniversary tribute to the Paris events of May 1968. We knew the music would be political, but we would need to jazz up the worthies at the Trafalgar Square end and pump subversive culture into the Long March if the demonstration itself was going to make a statement. We had been thinking about art and politics solidly for the last decade; we had the traditions, the ideas and the experience. Only this time we had the power to force the Left to relate to us. For we had been at intimate, permanent, fraternal loggerheads with those leaders of the revolutionary Left who were highly

Left: **TRB and Aswad summit meeting.** Below: **Trafalgar Square lights up.** Right: **Red stitches it up.**

Syd Shelton

political but only in the very narrow book-cultured sense. Laurie Flynn, then a journalist and enthusiast for *Socialist Worker*, now a tad less enthusiastic, puts this argument sharply:

> **The closet intellectuals** who lead London's revolutionary groups view themselves as highly sophisticated people but they are in reality superbly parochial. They think only about class, not about consciousness. They don't seem to understand that any meaningful socialism has culture not only at its core, but *as* its core. They are philistine about many things, none more so than music, having no conception of its position in the consciousness industries of our

time. Almost without exception, they refuse the novelty, the richness, the idiosyncrasy of their own experience, the sixties, preferring ancient algebras to serious reflection and troublesome thoughts.

And if culture was seen as just a superstructure or a bit on the side, then the politics were bound to be one-dimensional and inauthentic. For me, it is no answer to bleat on about media bias – colossal and impudent as it is – if the Left's own press imitates, badly, the graphic style of that medium. And aims itself at a leadership composed of hypothetical male, white, happily married union activists heavily into carpet slippers, Brylcreem and whippets – figures who bear very little relation to anyone in the modern working class and less to the authors. The working classes have many educational failings but they are adept, and experienced, at spotting hypocrisy. If socialism is transmitted in a deliberately doleful, pre-electronic idiom, if its emotional appeal is to working-class sacrifice and middle-class guilt, and if its dominant medium is the ill-printed word and the drab public procession, it will simply bounce off people who have grown up on this side of the sixties watershed and leave barely a dent behind it. Or so we used to argue. But now was a chance to prove in practice that things could be done differently.

After initial doubts, Paul Holborow, who combined orthodoxy with a genius for improvisation, spoke at packed ANL meetings round the country and raised money for fleets of coaches, forty-two from Glasgow, fifteen from Sheffield, a whole train from Manchester. In London RAR told the then-Tory GLC that we expected about 1000 people and the media that 100,000 were coming. Instead of the usual glorified Tannoy system, RAR's sound engineers were negotiating with the Pink Floyd for the use of a state-of-the-art rig which would be heard in Walthamstow and had one of the first computerised mixing desks. An RAR–ANL summit conference about the height of the stage was held in the Polar Bear in Chinatown, W1. RAR tape-recorded it and threatened to release the tape if there was any disagreement. The ANL sponsors came up with the necessary £12,000, which was taken across London to the stage builders in notes.

Tom Robinson persuaded EMI to donate several thousands of pounds and then sent an RAR purchasing committee to a novelties warehouse in Brixton to buy 10,000 whistles and 5000 eye masks. The Jewish show-biz people were terrific. 'They're not British, Mr Samuelson, they're Nazis. And could we borrow a generator for the Carnival?' And depending on mood, everyone enquiring was told by RAR that they had to come on stilts or as dragons or playing brass instruments.

Two weeks before Carnival, Joe Strummer rang up the studio and said the Clash wanted to come round and talk about joining the bill. Their manager, Bernie Rhodes, who imagined himself the Willie Müzenberg of Camden Lock, was in another world. 'Who are these Nazis anyway? You might just as well be the Anti-Pencil-Sharpeners.' But Strummer and Topper Headon stayed till late and their decision to play headlined the music press the following week.

But despite Peter Hain's work, the march and carnival were initially either ignored or sneered at by Fleet Street, who were making much play of the Right equals Left cliché, as if, as Orwell puts it, they couldn't see the difference between rats and rat poison.

At 2.0 am on the night before the demonstration, a group of RAR stalwarts, including Tasmanian journalist Phillip Brooks and the New York poet and club doorman Haowi Montag, who inhabited a labyrinthine eighth-floor squat in

'There may come a day when passports will be redundant and checkpoints obliterated so that people of all colour can move freely from one end of the Earth to the other. I'm of the conviction, if ever that dream came true we would hear of no more wars and inter-racial and religious violence. I have been a trade unionist for 54 years. We had coloured men in the branch as far back as 1932. Perhaps you don't know a coloured girl was instrumental in saving my life in hospital or that the bloke who drove my bus coloured and the chap who gave me a cheery good morning. By the way, I'm non-sectarian, non-racial.'
'A Cockney', writing to the *East London Advertiser*

Trafalgar Square viewed from the podium.

Charing Cross Road, began to hear crowds chanting through the downpour. And by 6.0 am the following morning there were already 10,000 people in Trafalgar Square. By midday the sun was out and the whole lot were there – Old Left, New Left and Left Out, punks and hippies and skins, vicars and trade unionists, blacks, browns and pinks. It was certainly the biggest anti-fascist rally since the thirties.

And it looked beautiful. Trafalgar Square, the site of so many grey occasions, was raked with colour. Yellow ANL roundels, punk pink Rock Against Racism stars, Day-Glo flags oscillating in approval to the speeches. Giant papier-mâché heads of the National Front leaders, streamers, Lone Ranger

Left: **Papier-mâché Adolf.** Centre: **Anti-racist stilt man.** Right: **The police out in front.**

masks, steel bands and reggae and punk from flat-bed trucks, and thousands upon thousands of plastic whistles formed slipstreams of colour and sound. It was a positive, joyous carnival against the No Fun, No Future philosophy of the NF.

'People were dancing in the streets for the whole of the six miles, that was the mode of transport. They kept coming,' Joanna Rollo recalls. The civil servants' trade union brought a dragon, the march was led by a clown on stilts and there was music all the way. Roger Law's giant heads of Hitler, Webster and Tyndall were rolled along the gutters.

Outside a couple of pubs near Brick Lane, there were a few Fronters with their mates, the sort of beer-gut and Page Three brigade who have an *I love virgins* sticker in the back of their off-brown resprayed Rover saloon and two kids whom they hit. They had come for a good laugh at the do-gooders. Three hours and 100,000 demonstrators later, the smiles were well and truly wiped off their faces and their bloated egos had evaporated into the swill at the bottom of their glasses.

Outside St John's, Bethnal Green, the vicar stood with his violet cassock and ANL badge telling everyone: 'This is a great sight. This is a proud day for Bethnal Green.' For three quarters of a mile back up the length of the Bethnal Green Road, it was blocked solid with people.

Back in Victoria Park, the man from the GLC had finally sussed the huge rig and stage. But he was also chuffed that something exciting was happening in his park and he was presented with a bottle of malt whisky, introduced to the bands and convinced that it was all right. The police had given up trying. There was no communication whatsoever between the now fortified stage, sodden by twelve hours of driving rain, and the marchers. 'So by one of those

'It is a matter at once for hope and for despair that there are so many young, creative, intelligent people without work or prospects here: despair that the social set-up has cut them off from opportunities and expression: hope that their very exclusion from a society so ugly and fruitless as ours now is will one day allow them to renew it, through new activities and new structures.'
Ann Dummett

Left: **Deflated Front fans in Bethnal Green Road.** Centre: **On foot.** Right **Mobile music.**

Left and right: **Steppin' to the music.**
Centre: **RAR propaganda.**

coincidences you look back on with awe,' Roger Huddle remembers, 'the sun broke through at 1.30 exactly and although there were only a few hundred people in the park, I introduced X-Ray Spex. As they came on, the march started to flood through the park gates.'

As the park slowly filled up one could float through three generations of the Left. At the outskirts there were couples who might have met at a Workers Educational Association summer school on the modern novel, had been in the front of Trafalgar Square when Bevan spoke against the Suez invasion, and sometimes did the *New Statesman* competition on Sunday. Their sensible footwear had been learnt on the Aldermaston march but the thermos flask and binoculars came from bird-watching outings. The only speaker they had managed to hear was Tom Robinson and he reminded them a bit of the young Anthony Wedgwood Benn.

Between them and the middle ground were ex-hippies, fire-eaters, clowns and people from the *Militant* giving out leaflets explaining why you should not support the ANL. The middle was the generation of 1968, listening knowledgeably but not at all sure who was playing. They had henna on for the occasion even if it did remind them of a commune they'd rather forget and they were slightly worried about the whereabouts of their eight-year-old whom they had arranged to hand over to its other single parent by the inflatables. They had quite liked Tony Benn's speech, which had reminded them a bit of the young Tony Cliff.

Between them and the 200-yard-deep sea of pogoing punks was a mud moat studded with upturned cider bottles and brown-sodden socialist newspapers. The front-line punks had been on amphetamine for days and were

Right: **On the long march to Victoria Park.** Below: **Arriving.**

Anti Nazi League

ROCK AGAINST RACISM

The Clash on stage.

Poly Styrene.

Tom Robinson
Mick Jo

Syd Shelton

Chris Schwarz

Chris Schwarz

'The imaginary is that which tends to become real.'
André Breton

Holding the fence together.

Chris Schwarz

Syd Shelton

Unknown

Above: **X-Ray Specs.**
Below: **Mick Jones and Danny Kustow.**

Syd Shelton

living for this moment. This was their Woodstock and their Grosvenor Square. When Red strode out in his Mr Oligarchy cape and bellowed, **'This ain't no fuckin' Woodstock,'** it was even better. The punks didn't like any of the speakers but knew exactly what the music was saying.

X-Ray Spex sounded lovely outdoors, the Clash thrashed rather inaudibly (one of their management had insisted, against advice, on remixing the very sophisticated board and in the process of trying to turn up the sound he lost most of their volume), Steel Pulse were stately, musically outstanding and their dignity and black pride flowed into the whole park.

There had been an argument in RAR about who should play last. It was the Clash who had pulled the hard punks. But they were still infantile, egocentric and in love with rock and roll which means *I'm somebody and you're nothing*. No one much minded Strummer's camp Red Brigade T-shirt but it was a shock to find they were filming their own home movie, *Rude Boy*, without mentioning it. Tom Robinson was the final choice for finale band and focused the day flawlessly and selflessly. That he ended with an anthem to gay pride instead of a rock-and-roll strut was more moving, for all three generations, than he realised.

Record Mirror called it 'the first truly positive musical event of 1978'. *New Musical Express* pontificated that 'Rocking Against Racism was the only way to relieve a social conscience without interrupting the party'. The day inspired the nearest RAR ever got to a manifesto, which ended:

> **It's pathetic that** it's taken the Front to bring us together. Maybe more people will still vote for the Front's respectable face, out of ignorance or hatred or sheer bloody-mindedness. But our determination, our solidarity, our music is growing faster. Yes, Lewisham

NORTHERN CARNIVAL

"FIRST ROCK, MEANING ROCK MUSIC, ROCK MUSIC AGAINST RACISM.
SECOND, ROCK LIKE YOU'RE ROCKIN', LIKE DANCING AGAINST RACISM.
THEN ITS LIKE ROCK, LIKE STONE, HARD LIKE A PEBBLE. PUT IT IN THE WATER
AND NOTHING CAN WASH IT AWAY! Selwyn, Steel Pulse

**ALEXANDRA PARK
15 JULY 1978
MOSS SIDE
ROCK AGAINST RACISM**

THE FALL STEEL PULSE
JOHN COOPER CLARKE
THE BUZZCOCKS
GRAHAM PARKER
CHINA STREET
EXODUS

and the Gate had to be done; the harder they come, the harder they fall. But it's great that musicians and actresses and footballers aren't too high and mighty to speak out too. And best of all, tens of thousands of unknown, unfamous people have worn a badge or won an argument or moved a resolution, or put on a gig. Roots, radicals, rockers, reggae: we come together today.

The summer of 1978 became carnival summer; by the autumn a staggering 400,000 had rocked against racism. There was Manchester's Carnival of the North (Buzzcocks, China Street, Exodus and Steel Pulse again) preceded by a Graham Parker and the Rumour *rehearsal* which was the band's best ever open-air gig. The Manchester Parks Committee were enraged at the Parker concert and threatened to announce the cancellation of the Belle Vue Carnival. Paul Holborow saved the situation by agreeing that a senior official of the council should be present throughout to ascertain its rehearsal status. He watched with a cynical smile and gave the go-ahead in a crowd of 3000 as the compere, the North West Spanner actor Ernie Dalton, also with a cynical smile, insisted at the end of every song, 'Don't clap too hard, this is only a rehearsal.'

The Carnival of the North was the biggest political march since Peterloo; then it was copied by Brixton's Carnival Two (Stiffs, Misty, Aswad, and Elvis Costello and the Attractions) in September. Carnival Two was only five months after Victoria Park but light years more sophisticated; the sound was immaculate, the stage space-age and the backstage arrangements almost civilised. Gerry Fitzpatrick, who could organise everything from a riot to refreshments

Red Saunders

Steel Pulse leaving the stage.

ROD STEWART

I think Enoch Powell is the man. I'm all for him. This country is over-crowded. The immigrants should be sent home. That's it.

Syd Shelton

for 100,000, co-ordinated two fields of carnival village. Crisis, the Ruts, the Members, Belt and Braces Band and China Street played off flat-bed trucks powered by petrol generators. Stiff Little Fingers, newly arrived from Northern Ireland, opened instead of Sham 69, who had pulled out only days before the gig amid rumour and gossip. And when Jake Burns took off his specs and donned his leathers he transmogrified himself into one of the most stinging vocalists and fiery guitarists punk ever possessed. The Stiffs' incendiary songs brought in the Irish dimension so important to any movement against racism in Britain, even though Burns denounced troops out. But better, they did punk homage to Bob Marley's classic *Johnny Was*.

Above left: **Brinsley Forde and Aswad, Brockwell Park.** Below left: **Stiff Little Fingers.** Below: **Elvis Costello and an Attraction.**

Syd Shelton

'Three highballs and I think I'm St Francis of Assisi.'
Dorothy Parker

92

Misty were joyous that day, lilting and weaving into the rhythms so evocatively that for a half-hour Brockwell Park was transferred to the Jamaican mountains by their open, rural, spiritual music. Behind the stage the Saxon Sound System was belting away and up in the jazz tent Gorgeous George Melly was barrelhousing on about the anti-racist bags under his canary's eyes.

But it was the arrival at the microphone of a haggard-looking Jimmy Pursey that brought the crowd of 150,000 to their toes. In a voice hoarse with emotion he bellowed, 'All this week you've probably read a lot of things about me and Sham 69. We've been dictated to. Last night I wasn't going to come. Then this little kid said to me, "You're not doing it because all your fans are NF." They said I ain't got no bottle. But I'm here. Nobody's going to tell me what I should or should not do. I'm here because I support Rock Against Racism.'

'Reggae is sharing a weight.'
Bunny Wailer

n exhausted, defiant Jimmy
ursey makes his stage
eclaration at Carnival Two.

Elvis Costello and the Attractions bounced on stage, saying, 'Welcome to he black and white minstrel show, 'ow about jumping up and down against acism?' And Brinsley Forde of Aswad was impressed. 'This is ire, ire that here's so many people today,' he was saying during 'Natural Progression', efore starting his chant of 'One love, one aim, one destiny'. King Sounds, ho was MCing at the time, skimmed green vinyl 12-inch records into the udience, and in the setting sunlight Aswad seemed to shimmer. A coal-tained miner in full equipment from Pye Hill colliery in Nottinghamshire nswered the sentiments from the musicians beautifully with his handwritten lacard: *We're black too some of the time. In our hearts we're all the same.*

Top: **Misty warm it up.**
Middle: **Red and Jo,
Carnival 2 comperes,
in Day-Glo boiler suits.**
Bottom: **Ruth, left
holding the tripod.**

New Society wrote:

The three great carnivals, Victoria Park, Brockwell Park and Belle Vue, Manchester, were extraordinary *moments* of popular protest. And while the Anti-Nazi league organisation in the trade unions was ideologically effective as counter-propaganda, the people mobilised on the demonstrations and the pickets were the younger people coming to anti-racism and anti-fascism through the *'moral'* perspectives offered by Rock Against Racism and the popular music culture . . . by members of a generation deeply influenced by sexual politics and by working-class people in the inner city areas, who found in multi-racialism and cosmopolitanism a culture to be defended rather than eradicated.

But Carnival Two showed that the National Front were sharpening their tactics. They had called a march in the Brick Lane area for the same day and announced it with only two weeks' notice. To cancel the carnival would have been organisationally impossible and would have given the NF a victory on a plate. The counterplan was to divert a sizeable section of the march to tackle the Front's efforts (they only managed to turn out 250 marchers but had enormous police protection). But as Holborow now puts it, '**We collectively bungled it.**' The transport logistics were not worked out and the anti-fascists who did attempt to block off the Front in Brick Lane were demoralised and easily pushed about by the belligerent police presence. The Front were harassed but not stopped and by the time reinforcements had arrived by Victoria Line from Brixton, the NF had dispersed.

Another of the drawbacks of the big carnivals was the time spent wading through the rubbish of rock-and-roll management who had not only moved into punk and collared it but had persuaded themselves they were the real stars. Managers took hours of precious time. The small fry were simply obnoxious. Richard Boon, the manager of the Buzzcocks, noisily told everyone backstage at the Northern Carnival, '**If this is the revolution, I don't think much of it.**' Michael Dempsey, manager of the Adverts, was as nice as pie when he wanted his band on the bill but warned other bands about '**Trotskyist manipulation**' behind our backs, and Dire Straits' manager vetoed a promised and desperately needed loan lest it be spent on guns. Even the sympathetic ones were naive about politics and we had to spend hours patiently explaining the basics. The Clash's Bernie Rhodes insisted that we'd have to be

Below left: **The best-dressed march in town.** Below centre: **Drag queens welcome the march.** Below right **Brixton gays against the Nazis**

armed before they'd join us — Sten guns in Knightsbridge were fine but he was scared of the coppers in the East End.

There was strong feeling in RAR that the big gigs were in danger of sticking to a safe formula and getting less political in the process. Much more energy, especially by Kate Webb and Jayne Harrison in the RAR office, was spent in helping set up smaller, more local outdoor gigs. Kate argued that although the Sex Pistols had blasted a way through the business, the bands that had been inspired by punk had simply headed for the bright lights of London. Isolated from their roots and their audience, they had fallen straight into the record-

Below: **Elvis in polka dots.** Above right: **Watching the invasion.** Below right: **Black and white unite.**

Syd Shelton

Syd Shelton

'If Charlie Parker had been French, they'd have had a monument built for him over there.'

Miles Davis

ompany velvet claws and the American-tour syndrome. But if punk was dead, Kate insisted in 1978,

RAR didn't die, far from it — we've gone from strength to strength. Why? Because we didn't depend on the *system*. It wasn't Harvey Goldsmith who put on some of the best bands to the biggest audiences earlier this year in the Carnivals, but a handful of music ans who knew no more about promoting concerts than you do. But RAR's not just about big band spectaculars. There are now fifty-two RAR groups putting on RAR gigs up and down the country. If you want to find out what RAR is really about, if you're sick of having nothing to do and nowhere to go to see live

NAZiS are No Fun — ROCK AGAINST RACISM

Tom Robinson, Barry Forde and Dambala's lead guitarist, Ally Pally.

Syd Shelton

Malcolm Owen and the Ruts, Dominion, Southall.

Misty on time, Cambridge.

Junior fans, Jackson Lane Community Centre.

Deptford Fun City.

DEPTFORD

Red Saunders

Bob Helm

TH No 8.

Sheffield RAR gig. Andy and Leon. Above right: Wicked sounds at the RCA, London.

Misty outside the Dominion, Southall.

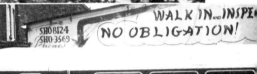

WALK IN AND INSPECT NO OBLIGATION!

Ranking Roger of the Beat, Birmingham Mecca.

Crisis, Harrow.

National Abortion Campaign demonstration against restrictive legislation.

Red and Roger, unrepentant mods, Clissold Park, London.

music, if you hate the Front or if you're just a certified lunatic write to us and we'll either put you in touch with your nearest RAR group or show you how to go about starting your own. There's a circular every fortnight and a gig guide to help you do it. We can't – it's up to you.

In creating a new culture it was the little, local gigs that mattered. Like Southall's in July 1978. Southall had some of the prettiest elms and meanest councillors in London. 'There was much hard bargaining with the local authority whose representative was unnecessarily obstructive and negative,' reported the official programme, produced by the *Other Ealing Gazette* for the many local organisations who put together the festival. 'Well, they said they'd have to arrest us if we used electricity,' pondered Chris of Misty. 'But there's going to be rather a lot of us.'

There were about 3000 comfortable, urban allsorts, inner city multi-racials, merry Marxists – the writing on their wall. Sikh elders smiled into their goatees. A line of West Indian girls swayed to the Mighty Metronome Sound. Skins with RAR badges plotted fanzines, a Sikh youth strode past with a brace of London Pride cans hooked on his index finger. A dread on pedals swerved through a parade of punks. Little stalls did brisk business: badges, tracts, ethnic snacks, Girls Unite! (an Asian women's group). It said *Stop the Nazis* on the litter bin and someone had sold a copper an ANL badge. A very serious game of cricket was going on in front of the toilets where the graffiti read *Condemned of Hounslow* (a band, not a hospital) and *I'm in a Rut*. The man from *Militant* hadn't sold a copy. He was the most impassive person there. There were a lot of smiles, genuine ones. Not a lot of fussing or overdoing it. Just easy, working it out together. It was a new sort of England being born, zippers and turbans and dub, as another England waited to die.

The Ruts were lovely and loved. Malcolm Owen went delicately berserk on the little, wobbly stage. Misty were hard as paving stones. One mike only for Puckie, Duxie and Antoinette, shared with Rankin' Reggie with his diddy stick and tracksuit and the ever lonesome Bongo Dannie. A hard, fast mix was courtesy of Chris, in his perpetual white trenchcoat, a detective of sound. The punks were captivated, the West Indians proud, the Asians interested. Misty's song *Judas Iscariot* just burnt and burnt. Misty had it – militant in a way the newspaper seller didn't seem to understand.

Top: **Misty at Southall Carnival.** Above: **Malcolm Owen of the Ruts.** Bottom: **RAR skins.**

By 1978 the electoral advance of the NF had faltered, but the business of being positively anti-racist was as urgent as ever . . . and as complicated. In *Temporary Hoarding* we tried to give out some information about how racism is all tied in with lousy housing and the dole and police brutality and self complexes. How it is knotted up in a thousand years of conveniently forgotten British history. How the industrial revolution was bankrolled by the slave trade and the plantation system, India was the launching pad for Britain's eighteenth-century Asian empire, and penetration of Latin America and the Far East paid for Victoria, Queen of Babylon, to rule the waves.

Vivien Goldman, the intrepid reggae critic, smuggled us back a tape of Peter Tosh's oration at the One Love reggae concert in Kingston. Said Tosh, whose lethal *Equal Rights* album seemed to have overtaken Marley in political edge, 'When Columbus and Henry Morgan and Francis Drake come up dem were just pirates but now dem put dem in a reading book and give us observation that we must look up and live the life of and the principles of them pirates. So the youth know fire dem guns like Henry Morgan, same way, fa now the shitstem have fe change.'

PETER TOSH

GUN COURT

Young Peter Tosh

HEAD OFFICE

The real high point of the show all that Manley/ Seaga/Marley three-step was cheese for the cameras . . . Peter Tosh's set left everyone in shock-nobody had expected that he would come and blow the stage apart, demolish the concept of the show and replace it with a truer vision. Peter's band-Words, Sound & Power—are the definitive late 70's reggae sound, as the Wailers were for the previous decade. The classic rhythm section, Robbie Shakespeare (bass) Sly Dunbar (drums) Ex-Wailer Al Anderson chipping through sparse lead guitar, helped out for the show by Mickey Chung, looking like a beached Chinese whale. Skullys shards of percussion. Soul Syndicate's Keith Stirling & In Crowd's Robert Lin doubled on keyboards. Peter plays a chiming chaka rhythm guitar. the words say it so read the transcript. You'll just have to imagine that you're listening to an orator so powerful he'd sway a statue of queen Victoria. A special merit award to Robert Shakespeare, who almost upstaged Peter—if that's possible—with his warlike lunges across the stage, thundering his bass

Militant,/me boss! The SUN & MOON of Reggae Igzabieher 400 Years Stepping' Razor HAIL RASTAFARI! Hail the father out loud, make lightning flash Its Words Sound & Power that bring down the barriers of oppression & drive away transgression & rule equality. Well right now fe a long time, 4,400 years and the same mucky master business & black inferiority & white superiority rule this little black country with our lives. Well I & & come with earthquake, lightning and thunder to ease barriers of oppression, drive away transgression and rule equality between humble people . . . Funeral after nerve jangling solos from slicing rhythm guitar (Peter) & percussion Peter said: 'Stand here at what dem seh call Peace Concert. I man never love come in it, you know why? It was a Peace Concert & our left wing people realise what the word Peace means eh? You see, most intellectual people in society think the word Peace means coming together. Peace is the diploma you get in the cemetery, seen? On top of your grave. Here lies the body of John Stokes, rest in peace. Seen? So you can imagine how defective peace is. This is an *intigration* concert, seen? Where black people come together fe get seh. well, something of a destructive element between I & I. What separates I & i

On the march against the NF in Birmingham.

'Nobody expects juju to conquer overnight. Rock music is roving around just now, and whoever grabs it will make the next pop music — it's Africa's turn now.'
Sunny Ade

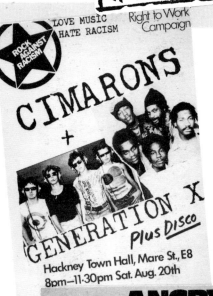

LOVE MUSIC HATE RACISM — Right to Work Campaign

ROCK AGAINST RACISM

CIMARONS + GENERATION X

Plus Disco

Hackney Town Hall, Mare St., E8
8pm–11.30pm Sat. Aug. 20th

ANGRY AND ON THE DOLE

MARCH for the RIGHT TO WORK

From Mozambique, RAR was sent a 'letter of support for our British brothers and sisters involved in "Rock Against Racism"'. The fifth-year students at the Samora Machel School said simply: 'Although our situations are different, two things link us, our age and our struggle against racism.'

Especially after an RAR-supporting band offended many women in the audience of a Brighton gig, RAR also tried to tackle sexual chauvinism in rock and roll, an enormous, vital task. We went through the usual arguments about feminism being divisive and similar rubbish, and at an RAR conference in Central Poly there was a serious and thoughtful discussion with members of Aswad about the Rastafarian attitude to women. *TH* argued that:

It is not enough to take a stand against one form of repression – the exploitation of the blacks – if they are going to subscribe to another – the degradation of women. But if anyone wonders why RAR doesn't simply ban all bands that are in the slightest bit sexist, the answer is (1) we would hardly have a band left on our books; (2) we hope that bands who don't normally have their sexist material challenged at ordinary gigs will benefit from doing an RAR gig and being confronted with feminist opposition. They deserve all they get!

RAR once again linked up with the Right to Work march, which in 1978 began in the occupied Bethnal Green Hospital and passed through Brixton on its way to the Brighton TUC. The march was entitled *Anger on the Road* and the punk band Crisis led it off. Misty gave a real roots welcome at Electric Avenue, Belt and Braces Band entertained at Crawley, and Patrick Fitzgerald, the Piranhas and a Skateboarders Against Racism rampage greeted the marchers to Brighton. The aim was to put 'the Big Heat on the TUC with the Brighton rock'. Our reasoning for the link between racism and unemployment was unsubtle but has proved accurate.

We're saying Mrs Thatcher will become the Queen of Babylon if we're not careful. Which is why the Carnival 2 in Brockwell Park. Which is why Anger on the Road. Because this is the March of the Dispossessed. And the angry kids from all over Britain will be there. Because racism grows out of unemployment. Like the Tories and the Labour are still trying to frighten people with the Numbers Game. And the Front are doing that basic thing that you haven't got

a job 'cos of the Blacks. And 'cos the Government and
the TUC ain't doing nothin about it. So the kids are
uniting and saying 'Why are you being hypocrites?'
to the TUC. Saying, 'Do something baldheads!'
And saying it, this year, with sounds.

The march itself was a success and inspiring to be part of. The problem was
that while the Right to Work campaign could provide an effective focus at a
time when the official trade-union movement was pathetically inactive, the
national rank-and-file workers' movements and workplace organisations
which could sponsor, sustain and generalise such activities were entering a
period of sharp decline. Still, when Tom Robinson entertained the weary
marchers by firelight with a plug-in electric guitar, it did feel as if the TUC's
serried baldheads were rattling to our righteous wrath. And when Tom got
John Deason, the Right to Work campaign's national secretary and a hard-
headed organiser, to mime to Lou Reed's most suggestive classics, the RAR
representatives were especially delighted.

The biggest target in the RAR and the ANL's calendar was the general
election finally called in May 1979, for which the National Front had planned a
national effort with candidates in every seat, party-political broadcasts tele-
vised on all channels, and the potential of a massive total fascist vote. After
long discussion it was decided to undertake RAR's biggest ever project, a
national road show which would select nightly programmes from a pool of
thirty bands and offer a nationally organised package and publicity which
local RAR supporters would be able to present with their own ideas and
expertise. This immense propaganda effort (far more ambitious than anything
the Labour Party attempted) resulted from a deliberate decision at RAR's
second national conference to scale down from the open-air carnivals of 1978
and get back to the roots, what *Temporary Hoarding*'s Lucy Toothpaste
called 'the real anarchy of the UK' – the RAR clubs. These local clubs had
some sort of existence in over fifty towns, putting on small-scale gigs, run by a
mixture of culture-conscious lefties and punk and Rasta kids. Like any
successful youth outfit, they were informal, a bit anarchic, and dependent on
friendship networks rather than membership cards. Which meant they were
sometimes shambolic and could create headaches for RAR central.

Sheryl Garrett, now music editor for the London weekly *City Limits*, went
along to Birmingham RAR as a schoolgirl of sixteen. 'Birmingham may be
Britain's second city but there are only about one hundred people alive in it.
And they were all there. We didn't have formal meetings, we just used to go to
people's flats and drink and talk either about what bands we should book next
for the RAR club at Digbeth Hall or the eternal argument about whether we
should let the skinheads in and argue with them or nut them on the door. I've
never been so certain of anything in my life,' she remembers, with faint
loathing.

The musicians were part of it, even the cynics like the languid Specials
vocalist Terry Hall who used to announce, '**Tonight we are rocking against
bacon and eggs.**' But if there was any racial aggro, he'd be the first to stop the
gig and get stuck in personally.

When the bands who expected something on the scale and professional-
ism of the carnivals ended up doing an ill-attended fund raising for the ANL
organised by the radical '**Jolly good show, up the revolution**' vicar, they took it
out on the national office. And absolutely committed bands like the Specials
and UB40 got distinctly weary of being denounced at parties because they

Syd Shelton

Saxa of the Beat.

101

hadn't been able to play some scout-hut benefit for Nicaragua at a week's notice.

So for RAR, the national tour was also part of firming up, 'Getting to know the faces behind the telephone numbers,' as Wayne Minter, who had joined John Dennis and Kate Webb as a full-time worker in the office, saw it. But the scale was still outrageous and the costs of bringing such political voltage to eighteen towns the length and breadth of the UK was prodigious for a group whose only source of income was badge and newspaper sales (RAR never received grant aid from any source).

The thirty or so bands rotated on the 1979 tour were approached on the basis of good music and commitment rather than Big Name. Nearly a third of the bands involved were offered major signings during the planning phase and outfits like the Ruts, the Gang of Four, the Mekons, Stiff Little Fingers, the

'Whoever heard of a revolution where they lock arms . . . singing ''We Shall Overcome''? In a revolution, you don't do any singing because you're so busy swinging.'

Malcolm X

Above left: **Tom Robinson and Tony James of Gen X, Ally Pally, London.** Above right: **Barry Forde, Leeds.** Left: **Syd on tour.** Right: **Andy Gill of the Gang of Four, West Runton.**

Left: **Stiff Little Fingers.** Right: **Babies against Nazism in Manchester.** Below left and right: **The Militant Entertainment tour at West Runton.**

Unknown

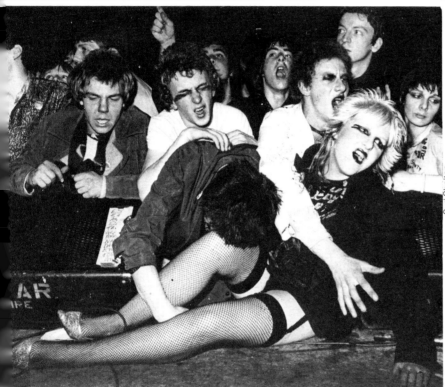

Syd Shelton

'We were generally happy in our lot – just to know that we were challenging one of the greatest empires in the world.'

T. Ras. Makonnen

Specials and the Leighton Buzzards were celebrated by the time of the tour.

On the road went four and a half tons of PA and lighting – a militant light show scudding images of Biko and Notting Hill Gate and Her Majesty with 'Scrounger' etched on her Royal Forehead – and a mobile RAR stall of badges and anti-racist propaganda. In place of honour was RAR's latest visual acquisition, a pink and blue flashing neon RAR star neatly boxed in shatterproof glass. Of course we said vote Labour, but with no illusions. RAR's real advice to the electorate – adapted from the female surrealist Mimi Parent – was 'Rock hard, life is deaf'. The point of bringing the cultural circus into town was to have the political argument and take the anti-racist message to the parts the other political organisations didn't reach. The bands shared hotels with the RAR organisers and every night there were intense talk sessions. Members of the bands helped out at the RAR stall and joined in the

arguments with the hostile kids who turned up at every gig.

'You see, I'm Jewish. And I'm with R.A.R. So you'd be killing me,' Geoff Den[] would carefully explain to the leader of a squad of skins with Union Jac[] badges. 'No, you're with the Leighton Buzzards, you do "Sunday Nigh[] Underneath The Palm Tree". You're all right, mate,' they would reply, and th[] RAR people would plough on until it was 'Tell you what, take the badges of[] come on in and have a pint'. And by the end of the evening the hecklers woul[] be up on stage cheering the dreadlocked Barry Forde to the echo. In Wales [] was the Hell's Angels and in Middlesborough, where Sid Vicious was big [] punks with neck padlocks and scars had been out leafleting the local footba[] stands the previous week.

In Norfolk bus drivers volunteered to drive RAR convoys from all over Ea[] Anglia, in Edinburgh, where an emergency second night was put on whe[] Stirling University cancelled at short notice, new posters were designe[] silk-screened and flyposted within hours of the news. And in Manchester, on[] of the four gigs RAR central had to cancel, two women in the Moss Side RA[] pulled together a last-minute local bill, packed the Poly on a Tuesday nig[] and produced one of the best concerts of the tour.

Red had adopted a teddy-boy persona and when not launching volunte[] Ruts fans headfirst into the human safety net of their friends in the audienc[] he was psycho-security: 'All right, lads,' he would bawl at the skinhead[] dismantling the speakers. 'No fucking bother, right?' With luck they would h[] back, 'Great, big fella.' If it got any worse, which it sometimes did, the tour wa[] in trouble.

The final extravaganza, in the huge floral hall of the Alexandra Palace [] Easter Sunday 1979, was a triumph. *Hi, this is your Alien Kulture* in eight-foo[]

Syd Shelton

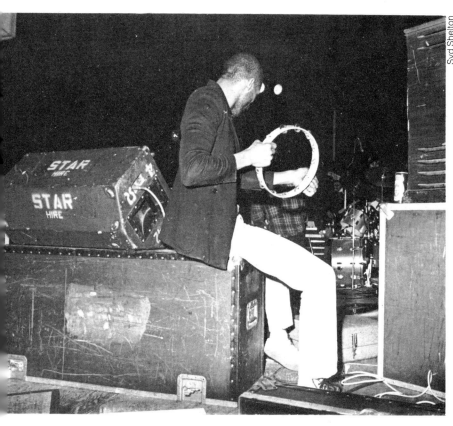

Syd Shelton

Clockwise from bottom left: **Vince and Smell, Leicester; Karen and Wayne, tour scouts; Mavrick Majestic Sound System, Leeds; Tom Robinson and Clarence Baker of Misty; Boxed-in beat; Militant punks.**

'Without oppression and without racism, you have no blues.'

Frantz Fanon

high Fablon letters was strung across a stage where fourteen different bands played over six hours, with Dambala, the Angelic Upstarts and John Cooper Clarke especially delightful. The Upstarts arrived with a personal goon squad, a pig's head and police siren as special effects, and a manager who had once been in the NF and had an alarming propensity to strip to his waist, clench every muscle in his torso and foam at the mouth if he felt affronted. On entry to the gig, he nutted two security people, told a very proper feminist from the Belt and Braces Band to suck his dick, and nearly ruptured his sterno mastoid muscles.

Over forty groups had stalls in a kind of political jumble sale at the south of the magnificent hall, and along its sides theatre groups like Beryl and the Perils and Broadside played between the stage acts. The veteran Glaswegian rocker, Alex Harvey, arrived on stage and led communal singing of Marley's *Small Axe*. John Cooper Clarke did a whole poem, *The Day My Pad Went MAD*, in seventeen seconds. Six hours into the all-day concert, backstage was awash with the crombied West Ham and Union Jack brigade, fortunately mostly in alcoholic coma. The stage itself was highly insecure and was only inadvertently cleared by the musicians massing for the final jam, which had Dambala, Misty, Barry Forde, the Ruts, some Upstarts and Tom Robinson happy at last.

The tour, billed as 'a show of anti-racist enthusiasm aimed at racialist candidates of whatever party', was the only live event in an election which, despite its ghastly outcome, was conducted in somnambulant style. After hanging glumly on to office through compromises, coalitions and repeated postponements, Callaghan finally ended five undistinguished years of Labour government.

Southall, 23rd April 1979: police on the pavement, public in the gutter.

Just before the election, on 23rd April 1979, police *'protecting'* a National Front demonstration in Southall managed in the course of their peace-keeping endeavours to kill a demonstrator, Blair Peach, inflict serious skull and genital injuries on thirty others, arrest over 750 people and systematically destroy a community centre. Joanna Rollo was in Southall that day.

I remember getting there quite early. It was raining. There were a lot of policemen from about 11.0 am and they soon started to shove the Asians around – they were just being pushed aside and into the gutter. The police were quite rough, doing their macho stuff, they were really aggressive, they were looking for trouble. And it just got heavier and heavier through the day. There was some feeling among the people leading the demonstration that the best thing to do was to try and keep people together and not move off anywhere because the police were getting so violent. There were demonstrators all over Southall and about 1000 of us lined up opposite the town hall. The police line was broken in several places. Then the police counter-charged and John Rose and I got pushed into a back alley. The police horses came down after us chasing us into people's front gardens. And this woman opens her front door shouting, 'Get out of my front garden, you'll damage the roses,' and there were the horses coming down with the

David Hoffman

truncheons out and we were getting well and truly beaten.

They weren't trying to stop people, they weren't trying to arrest people, they were trying to punish us. It was incredibly violent. I've never been on such a violent demonstration, anywhere in the world. You'd get banged on the head and on the shoulders and on the back. We were running gauntlets and they were just taking swipes at whoever they could. They were just riding people down. I'm always amazed only one person got killed.

Clarence Baker (of Misty and the RAR committee) came close to death with a fractured skull and spent a week in a coma. And in Blair Peach we lost someone the writer Ken Walpole described as 'one of the wittiest and loveliest friends we are ever likely to have'. The going was getting tougher. At the time *Temporary Hoarding* wrote:

Southall is special. There have been police killings before. There will be police riots again. But on 23rd April the police behaved like never before. The tactics of the colonies had come back home to suburban back streets of West London with their rows of parked Morris Oxfords and houses called Ivanhoe. To walk over the railway bridge that night was to walk through the valley of the wicked. Elders arrested coming home from the temple, kids rounded up back from football because the police had stopped the buses. The police were off the leash and on the hunt. When they crack Clarence's skull and put the boot into Chris's kidneys, we all feel the pain. When they mash up the People Unite PA every musician ought to hear the crunch of their feet.

The events in Southall and the near murder of a member of one of the most idealistic reggae bands in Britain stung the music world into action. Pete Townshend came on side, as we always knew he would, and the Clash yet again did their duty.

RAR took out the seats of the Rainbow Theatre in Finsbury Park for two days and, with Pete Townshend, Aswad, the Pop Group, the Enchanters, the Clash, the Members, the Ruts and a defiant Misty, raised £5000 for the Southall

'When I see an actual flesh and blood worker in conflict with his natural enemy, the policeman, I do not have to ask myself which side am I on.'

George Orwell

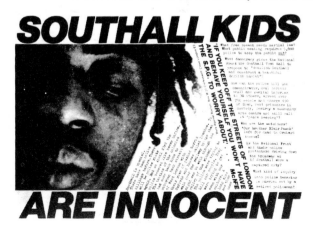

SOUTHALL KIDS ARE INNOCENT

Syd Shelton

Syd Shelton

Virginia Turbett

defendants. All the money went to the people hauled through the courts for the crime of protesting against National Front *'election meetings'* guarded by battalions of police, to the elders and kids and musicians brutalised in a police riot. And Joe Jackson took the initiative to organise his own concert for Southall, which raised £500.

A twenty-gig Dance and Defend tour raised more for the people arrested at NF election farces in Leicester and West Brom. The Gang of Four, the Mekons and Delta 5 plus 500 anti-sexist punks stirred it up on the massive TUC march against the Corrie Abortion Restriction Bill. And the word on the RAR telex was that groups were starting in Sweden, Holland, Japan, Italy and the USA. In West Germany there was Rock Gegen Recht, in Greenland a pro-RAR benefit album was issued, and in Belgium an RAR carnival led to an eight-hour battle with the police.

Top left: **Eel Pie Townshend.** Middle left: **Jayne at the Rainbow.** Bottom left: **Nicky Tesco of the Members** climaxes. Below: **Joe Strummer gets down at the Rainbow.**

Syd Shelton

Syd Shelton

Left: **Mick Jones and Paul Simonon of the Clash at the Rainbow.** Above: **Barry Forde.**

Malcolm Owen of the Ruts.

'The trouble with the Specials breaking up when they did is that we didn't follow through what we'd done with "Ghost Town". I feel we should have carried on, you have to follow something like that through.'
Jerry Dammers, Special AKA

Right: **Rhoda Dakar.** Far right: **Terry Hall and Lynval Golding, the original unbeaten Specials.**

Above: **Danny of Star Hire.** Top: **Ranking Roger.**

RAR's 1980 conference was hosted by the Birmingham group. Lesley Woods of the then unrecorded Au Pairs talked on sexism in music; the youth who was to metamorphose into the Beat's Ranking Roger did the toasting. If the RAR hard core was by 1980 showing signs of metal fatigue and pilot error, the post-punk music scene was changed by our existence. There was a return to escapism in music and apolitical egotism in rock journalism. But the Two-Tone bands with their racially mixed-up musicians and political dance music that ministered to head, heart and feet were like a logical culmination of the RAR funky-politics philosophy. And although it took time, the brilliant music from the Beat, UB40 and the Specials and their urgent, public and danceable stand against racism surpassed our wildest hopes. In February 1981 *Rock Against Racism's Greatest Hits* was issued on Virgin Records, the first ever LP done as a political benefit and the precedent for subsequent vinyl for Amnesty, CND, Greenpeace and Band Aid.

In July 1981 RAR held one of its best ever carnivals, entirely peacefully, in Leeds. On stage there were the Specials, the mighty Misty, the Au Pairs, and Barry Forde rocking again. The Leeds carnival was the youngest and most working-class carnival yet, with more black youth involved than ever before. Jerry Dammers described the Specials as 'a multi-racial line-up mixing different styles of music', but they were *Mad* magazine and bad taste Hawaiian shirts and Fay Fife hairdos too. Leeds was the Specials' finest hour with music merging into political feeling and vice versa, with neither ingredient adulterated. Looking over the vast crowd in Chapeltown, Neville Staples said, 'It's like a zebra crossing, black and white, black and white as far as you can see.' Revenge, not just against the racists but against all those elders and betters who said it couldn't happen, was sweet.

Syd Shelton

Lesley Woods, Brum chantreuse.

GOTTA KEEP ON KEEPING ON

Dan Jones

The 1979 general election is now remembered for the vote which delivered us to the mercies, and they are few, of Margaret Thatcher's era of office. But it was also a catastrophe for the National Front.

In the local elections in 1977 and 1978, their vote had begun to plummet, even in their imagined strongholds like Leicester (where it fell from 17 per cent to 5 per cent) and in Wolverhampton (where the fall was from 11 per cent to 3 per cent). But in the general election, projected as the breakthrough into national politics, they were humiliated, failing to retain a single deposit. And this reversal generated internal splits; Martin Webster, the chief NF organiser, was expelled and the Front divided into three rival organisations: National Front (Constitutional), National Front, and British National Party.

Part of the NF's problem was Mrs Thatcher. Its period of growth had been during the relatively liberal Tory leadership of Edward Heath. Thatcher's harsh line on immigration controls and clear identification with the traditions of white empire brought the racialist vote back into the Tory fold. But RAR and the ANL had hit hard and repeatedly at both NF organisation and electoral support.

Martin Webster, unsuccessfully defending himself in a libel case brought against him by Peter Hain, spoke eloquently and probably honestly in court about the impact of the Anti-Nazi League and RAR's campaign. Hain recalls:

> **He was still** extremely bitter and remarkably candid. The picture he gave, and he clearly believed it, was that prior to 1977, the NF were unstoppable and he was well on the way to becoming prime minister. Then suddenly the ANL was everywhere and knocked hell out of them. It obviously still hurt. He said that the sheer presence of the ANL had made it impossible to get NF members onto the streets, had dashed recruitment and cut away at their vote. It wasn't just the physical opposition to the marches, they had lost the propaganda war too.

If such a campaign as the ANL and RAR had not been launched in Britain, there is every reason to suspect that the mid-seventies electoral surge of the NF might have been sustained. The evidence is in France where Jean-Marie le Pen, now leader of Europe's largest movement of the extreme Right, advanced from a mere 0.2 per cent in the March 1982 local (cantonal)

> 'We shouldn't go down the American road of hard policing. When my children grow up I don't want them to turn to me and say "Why did you give us this kind of violent society, why does society hate the police?"'
> **Detective Inspector Wilfred Knight**

Syd Shelton

Vince and Smell, on the Militant Entertainment Tour.

elections via the 16.7 per cent by-election vote in summer 1983 in Dreux to a total of 2.5 million votes in the 1984 Euro-election, almost the same share of the vote as the Communists. The French NF now send eleven deputies to the European Parliament at Strasbourg where they form a fascist bloc with the Italian neo-Nazis. 'No doubt remains,' commented the newspaper *Le Monde* in March 1985, 'Le Pen has, as from now, become part of the French political landscape.'

This breakthrough cannot be wholly explained as a reversion to an old French tradition (obscured politically by Gaullism) of Vichy, Poujade and the OAS, or even by the impasse of Mitterrand's socialism. It has to be said that the organised French Left were too complacent about their traditional vote in the northeast, the Mediterranean ports and the inner cities and had really failed to fight racism alongside the immigrant workers. On the contrary, the French Communist Party had even initiated racist demonstrations in suburbs under its municipal control. So Le Pen's chirpy, *sportif* appeal and cunning sloganeering ('What are my policies? They are what you are thinking') were knocking on an opened door.

A Western European Left which does not seek to understand and then to tackle racism head-on is cutting its own throat. The loss of support from proletarian socialists who are sympathetic to racialist explanations (and there are still a few about) is better than endless equivocation, denial and ineffective compromise on this issue. Socialists have an honourable tradition to uphold, we must continue to insist that the ideas of national chauvinism and racial supremacy are foreign to working-class terrain and promptly repatriate them to those portions of the bourgeoisie where they and much other unwanted ideology were invented. And the way to do that is not by moralism from above but by direct action from below. Exactly as our dear godfather V. I. Lenin (the Soviet Lenin who loved Mayakovsky, Grosz, electricity, the cinema and explosive punctuation) advocated when he asserted that socialists 'must open the eyes of the people . . . teach them not to place trust in promises and rely on their OWN forces, on *their* OWN organisation, on *their* OWN unity, and on *their* OWN weapons alone'.

The ANL had shown that it could be done this way: the struggle on the streets could set the tempo and the politicians and celebrities support and generalise but not dictate to it. It demonstrated that an unrespectable but effective unity between groups with wide political differences (the SWP, the organisations of the black communities and the Labour Party) can reach and touch an audience of millions, not by compromise but by assertive campaigning and wholehearted use of modern propaganda. The alliance between the SWP, a Marxist party of a few thousand members, and the Labour Party, a reformist parliamentary party with 8 million voters, was less incongruous than it sounded. For a clear-cut common goal had been set – the decrease of the influence of the NF – even if the Labour Party's primary concern was the danger of losing marginal seats because of a high NF vote and the SWP's was to encourage people to consider the case for revolutionary social change by working-class direct action.

During one crisis on the steering committee of ANL, Paul Holborow remembers phoning Neil Kinnock, then one of the most active Labour MPs in the ANL. 'I really tried to explain,' he says, 'that there were really big differences between us but as far as I was concerned the ANL was an important organisation which we both from different points of view needed to support.' Very cold and calm. And Kinnock replied, 'Look, I don't really care what your political organisation is. As far as I'm concerned the ANL performs a

Syd Shelton

very important function for the Labour Party.'

In Holborow's view the revolutionary Left, especially in a period of political downturn, 'tends to lack self-confidence and retreat into a self-consoling sectarianism. But if your politics fit you can offer activity which is clear-sighted, never mind the scale. Then, to be honest, people don't start to quibble about the fine print.' But he notes that what made the ANL stick in the black communities was quite different. 'Voting patterns had nothing to do with it here, we had to prove we could effectively deal with the beast in our own white communities. Only then could we go forward as equal fighters with the blacks who had been contending with racism since they were two years old.'

Certainly in East London evidence of interracial working-class unity is more obvious than only five years ago. In the Assembly Hall where Generation X and the Cimarrons played after Lewisham, in the Christmas of 1984 I sat with black children in neatly plaited dreadlocks brought by their Rasta parents to listen to the uplifting chorale of the Mynyddrslwyn Male Voice Choir from South Wales singing in Hackney in support of the NUM. In the council chamber itself, an Anti-Deportation Campaign was launched in 1985 which brought together for the first time the Turkish community, who had campaigned for the Hasbuduk family, with Afro-Caribbean organisations and the Asian Centre. In the March 1985 celebrations which accompanied the renaming of the Dalston library after C. L. R. James, over 200 people, mostly Afro-Caribbean and some very young, listened with pride to Linton Kwesi Johnson's poems and an account by a leader of the Trinidad Oil Workers Union of C. L. R. James who organised the Africa Bureau with Padmore, bearded Trotsky in Coyaocan, organised sharecroppers in Missouri, hailed Nkrumah as the black Lenin in Accra and now has his name in lights in Dalston Lane.

Things move more slowly in Tower Hamlets and Newham. The slogan *Black and White unite and fight* has been often misused by bureaucratic white socialists who want blacks to cut their struggles out of white political cloth. But when white trade unionists march proudly alongside the brave young Sikh men and women who are fighting back against racism in E17, that is progress. And when Bengali mothers take to the streets of Whitechapel to join a mass march in support of a victimised white woman consultant obstetrician, the political leap is still greater.

In the baby clinics, the schools and the streets there has been a real shift of attitudes in East London over the last five years. It's not nowadays considered very clever to sneer at blacks. It's only fools who try to blame them for all that is wrong with life. The NF is, once again, ineffectual and its few remaining daubings over railway bridges and park walls have the air of very old dogs'

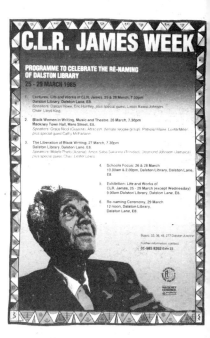

'Since 1789 the aristocracy of birth and the aristocracy of religion have been destroyed: but the aristocracy of skin still remains. That too is in its last gasp and equality has been consecrated. A black man, a yellow man, are about to join this Convention in the name of the free citizens of San Domingo.'

French Revolutionary Convention

The New Cross massacre: '13 dead, nothing said'.

'Maybe the real criminals in this society are not the people who populate the prisons . . . but those who have stolen the wealth of the world from the people.'

Angela Davis

Geldof, paying some back.

droppings. The fascists and their friends and apologists like the Fair Play (for whites) organisation have bungled opportunities such as the GLC evictions, over which the NF of 1976 would have built large campaigns. And the arson crisis in mid-1985 showed that the Sikhs of Newham have learnt lessons from Brick Lane in 1977, if the police have not. Whether it's down to Cyrille Regis the footballer, Tessa Sanderson the athlete, Norman Cowans the bowler, and Rankin' Miss P, Radio One's first black woman DJ, or to the bravery of the youth in Brick Lane, New Cross and the Uprising of 1981, there is a new respect abroad. The black experience is seen to be altering, educating and enriching the cultural identity of modern Londoners.

The joint resistance of the white, black and brown urban working class to the neglect and speculation which devour their communities may mark a new stage in the history of London labour.

Politics is not just about alliances, but the terms on which they are made. Without the post-electronic, youth-oriented input of RAR, the ANL alliance would have a lesser impact. Yet without punk, RAR in turn might well have been little more than what Kate Webb describes as 'a dominant, fairly egocentric group of artistic people – most of whom were of a different generation and experience to the RAR people "out there"'.

The lessons lie in the connections and political timing. The ideas, the cultural ingredients, the potential had been there for years but they could only be utilised in a genuine crisis. The endless subsequent attempts to use the RAR formula, whether Rock Against Inner Ring Roads or Rock for Jobs, have worked as fund raisers and crowd pullers but little else. On the other hand Bob Geldof's and Band Aid's brilliant fund-raising effort for Ethiopia, smug and Establishment as it often was, works politically because, like RAR, it is a practical response to a crisis conventional politics clearly can't handle.

There were plenty of loathsome aspects about the Live Aid concert jointly held in London and Philadelphia in July 1985, in particular the refusal to find space for black British bands who have contributed so much to the culture and had organised the first benefit for food to Ethiopia ten years earlier with a bill that included Bob Marley and the Wailers. Indeed, a rock concert can do little to reverse the casual destruction of the globe's ecology and the destructive results of forced cash-cropping for the West's vast craw. And most of the performers still seemed to think that all you need is love and heavy-metal poses, although the Thompson Twins' version of Lennon's *Revolution*, the Who's stunning *Won't Get Fooled Again*, Jagger and Bowie's wonderful camp homage to *Dancing In The Street* and, absurdly, Freddie Mercury's acoustic duo, all had anger and edge. But the rock and roll spirit of getting on and *doing* something, the audacious internationalism of the TV transmission and the way electronic audience could for once feel part of a culture that could act collectively, were all exhilarating.

The political problem was not that Live Aid failed to overthrow imperialism East and West (which it never intended) but it became so obsessed with Access card numbers it neglected its other declared intention, to really hammer the big powers' refusal of effective aid. Geldof was not *'too egotistic'* rather he was too easily steered from confronting Thatcher to having off-the-record dinner with the royals, partly because it was too much a one-man band. But it was moving to see our old adversary Eric Clapton on the right side at last and playing with such grace and fluidity, and Bowie, now the statesman of rock-come-of-age, dedicating *Heroes* to 'my son, your children and the children of the world'. Lefties who cough and sneer at this shift in rock-and-roll political consciousness have a corpse-sized lozenge in their throat. And the deny the influence the political Left has had in pioneering new sorts of links between music and politics. The real sadness was that neither Bob Marley nor John Lennon, who had both dealt so brilliantly in politics and music, could have been there.

RAR, with which Geldof and many other Live Aid musicians had been in contact in the seventies, was not just about beating the NF at the ballot box but a campaign to change attitudes within popular culture. Although RAR used music to get conventional anti-racist ideas across to a pop audience, we also hoped to change values in the music itself. Our aim was to become unnecessary by establishing an anti-racist, multi-cultural and polysexual feeling in pop music which would be self-generating, and to make politics as legitimate a subject matter as love.

After the assimilation of punk, it had seemed that the majority of chart pop

music was almost as politically bland, sexually conventional and morally empty as that which we endured in the mid-seventies or the early sixties. And much of the more experimental pop music being produced on surviving independent labels like Mute, Rough Trade and Factory was artistically feeble and politically incomprehensible.

But things were not quite as bad as the Duran Duran videos suggested. Whatever the follies of eighties pop, there has been no sign of overt racism from white musicians, a definite improvement. And a real political internationalism – reflecting the music's worldwide ingredients – was indicated when an artist like Peter Gabriel brought out his stunning tribute to Steve Biko with its sonorous and, to the South African regime, ominous refrain of candles and of flames. And still more when Gabriel bravely put his money behind the WOMAD pancultural music festival. In 1985 WOMAD brought General

Above: **The uprisings begin again, as traditional a British response to social crisis as royal romance.** Top right: **Himself, Robert Nesta Marley.**

FREE NELSON MANDELA!

SOLIDARITY WITH SOUTH AFRICAN AND NAMIBIAN POLITICAL PRISONERS!

Poster: David King

Twenty-three years in captivity.

I emptied my revolver among the yelling mass

✗

'Jesus told me only one thing – love ye one another. And don't judge each other.'
Little Richard

Public with the old Brum RAR skanker Ranking Roger together with Toots and the Maytals' classic Jamaican pop and the angry countrybilly attack of the Pogues and the Boothill Foot-Tappers, interspliced with samba musicians, African guitarists and Thomas Mapfumo's flaring folk chants and limbo, displaying, on a cold island in Essex, the astonishing range and interaction of musicians now based in Britain.

Racially and sexually mixed bands from Working Week to Culture Club are now two a penny. And in a mawkish kind of way, Stevie Wonder and Paul McCartney's paean to a multi-racial community established on the keyboard of a grand piano, *Ebony And Ivory* – an international smash-hit duet by two of the most successful musicians in the world – was highly effective. It is easy to be superior about this sort of MOR collaboration. But, as Kate Webb puts it, 'So many people bought the record because they wanted to have simple anti-racist messages expressed and they are not anywhere else in the culture.' And the Special AKA's buoyant *Nelson Mandela*, inspired by Jerry Dammers' listening to South African bands at a London Against Racism, GLC-sponsored open-air concert, was so effective because of its simplicity.

The potent idea that pop music can be about something more than mere entertainment has remained and deepened. Live Aid above all but even Wham! miming for the miners, Bruce Springsteen's hefty donation to the Women Against Pit Closures campaign, and the joint version of *I'll Never Walk Alone* to raise money for the victims of the Bradford football stadium fire in June 1985, all represent a wider recognition of the social power popular music can have which goes back to RAR and the early days of punk. The music is often tinsel-weight but the projects represent a huge advance on the take-the-money-and-run pop mentality.

Optimism about rock music must be steeped in realism. It was saddening but predictable that Mick Jones of the Clash said of the 1981 uprisings, 'They should have had a little more patience,' and that the punks who thrashed through *I'm So Bored With The USA* should disappear across the Atlantic in search of FM market penetration. And demoralising that Julie Burchill should progress from the streets of New Cross to pieces on the loathsome working classes for the *Tatler*, apparently imagining that her age-old excuse for betrayal, '*I know, I'm one of them*', is some newfangled cry of defiance. But these inevitable defections are more than compensated for by the consistency of Elvis Costello, especially when he plays *Shipbuilding*, *Oliver's Army* and *Clowntime Is Over* in succession and issues records like *Pills And Soap* which for political lyricism stands comparison with the work of Auden before religion and monogamy got him.

Other punk originals, like Paul Weller, are producing better, musically more complex and emotionally sharper music now than in 1977, and Joe Strummer, Ian Dury and Tom Robinson, who have needed to hibernate, show no sign of stagnation or defeat. New talents like Billy Bragg, the Redskins and Ben Zehaniah are, in truth, a lot better than their equivalents in the punk heyday. Bands like Misty in Roots, Aswad, Steel Pulse and Bovelle's Dub Band continue, almost unnoticed by official culture, to produce outstanding and original music.

And it was significant that pop musicians refused to support the pocket jingoism of the Falklands expedition. The astute business weekly, the *Economist*, argued hopefully in June 1982, that the war might serve as a 'sort of cultural revolution' to the 'younger generation': 'Colonel "H" Jones, killed, General Jeremy Moore, alive. Both men a bit more handsome and heroic than Mr David Bowie.' But, as the Marxist critic Ian Birchall delightedly pointed out to the magazine a year later, 'This week in the charts the aforesaid Mr David Bowie has the best-selling single record in Britain and the best-selling long-playing record. You must feel very disappointed.' Birchall could have added that the single *China Girl* was described by Bowie, not entirely flippantly, as an analysis of imperialism. And that the nasty, profitless little war produced no pop-musical jingoism but instead, in *Shipbuilding* by Elvis Costello and *Between The Wars* by Billy Bragg, classics of anti-militarist scepticism.

Part of the rock-and-roll mentality was Thatcherite before Mrs T. was heard of but, overall, pop music has been surprisingly resistant to the Self-Servative mentality. Punk was a one-way valve: it is now impossible for pop to revert completely to the old apoliticism and be taken seriously. And when the political movement which punk expressed so incisively ebbed, there was by that time enough musical excellence, lyrical originality and musical intelligence to sustain progress.

Perhaps the best evidence of a new – or perhaps very old – social awareness among pop musicians was the range of musical support for the miners' strike, from Sade through Test Department, Misty and Mick Harding to the furious falsetto of Bronski Beat in the remarkable *'Pits and Perverts'* gay fund-raising ball. Eventually, even two of the Rolling Stones, who have given so little back to the culture that created them, supported the miners, and the dreaded Sting wrote a song about the economics of coal mining. And when Tom Robinson introduced a delegation of Welsh men and women from the mining community who had come to thank the gay movement for its sympathy and financial support to the biggest ever Gay Pride demonstration in London in June 1985 and the loudest roar of the afternoon hit the air, it must have meant a lot more than those uneasy *Glad To Be Gay* singalongs.

Yet only five years before, when RAR got 999's following to put their 10p pieces into the firemen's helmets, it was a novelty for pop musicians to support an industrial dispute, and gay people were *still*, to most miners, *just* a bunch of queers.

Watching the revolutionary musician Thomas Mapfumo and his band delight a 100 Club ram-packed with white and black Londoners in 1985, I had forcibly to remind myself that five years ago there was no Zimbabwe, no London club with a fifty-fifty black-white mix, and English interest in the wonders of African music didn't go much beyond the back counter of Sterns in Tottenham Court Road. And what a political journey has been made from the days when Linton Kwesi Johnson had to write his scornful poem *Independent Intervenshun* to his deeply felt *Reggae Fe Peach*, a tribute to his fellow socialist Blair Peach on the 1982 *Bass Culture* album.

The process of stylistic interaction and enrichment is now so accepted in

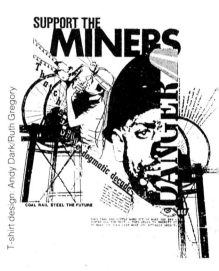

T-shirt design: Andy Dark/Ruth Gregory

Linton Kwesi Johnson.

British music that it no longer matters whether it's a white Brummie playin(
intricate dub or a black East Ender with that exquisite soul voice. It's still tru
that black UK musicians of phenomenal ability and proven artistic achieve
ment, like Aswad, Misty, the Cimarrons, Steel Pulse and Matumbi, are denie
the exposure which is automatically lavished on record-company-concocte
chart fodder. But there is, in the UK more than anywhere on the atlas, a hig
level of creative interaction between black and white traditions.

There is nothing inherently musically or politically progressive about in
migration. North America is a clear example of how a medley of racisn
ferocious individualism and massive immigration can be compatible. Pete
Sedgwick, the most original post-war Marxist in Britain, once wrote of Ne
York as 'this vast multi-cellular pulp-colony, which academics call a collectic
of sub-cultures: Italian, Japanese, Negro, Puerto Rican, student-hip, meths
incontinents, ex-Jewish, and the suburban Wild West bar on our corner whe
the people actually regard me as having long hair. They aren't sub-culture
because there isn't any superordinate culture the next stage up, all there is
this coexisting mass of globules.' Whereas although modern London is
sexual, musical and political frontier town wide open to an extraordina
ethnic mix, of all the European metropolises, we still hold intact enough of
common popular culture in long-standing political institutions and traditio
to guarantee meeting and thence interaction of constituent cultures. Whic
makes modern London so different from America or mainland Europe an
despite all Thatcher's efforts, such a cosmopolitan, creative and non-globu
city.

Afrika Bambaataa and the Bronx hip-hop crews he brought over in the spri
of 1985 were impressed by the lack of racism in the clubs, the ease of artis
crossover and the facilities that the municipality of London was prepared
put at kids' disposal (**'The kids back home wouldn't believe your Sh**
Theatre. They don't let us within a half mile of places like this in Manhattar
For whatever one's reservations about Ken Livingstone's GLC, it prised op
the South Bank, the concert halls and public parks and gave them over
popular performance. When Ranking Ann was toasting free on the stage
the Queen Elizabeth Hall, Misty were making the County Hall car pa
shudder, ragas tintinnabulated through the Purcell Room and ice-cream va
sounded outside, one began to hear what a socialist city might sound like.

It is at these international meeting and mutation points that the creat
advances will be made and our future musical and political identities will
discovered. And this process restores to popular music exactly the so(
dimensions which commerce seeks to strip from it. Definitions must chan

Left: **Elastic hip hop.** Below: **Twin mods.** Bottom: **Peter Tosh and an admirer.**

radio music presenters like Charlie Gillett, John Peel, Peter Clayton, David Roddigan and the late Alexis Korner are not mere disc jockeys but musical educators. Record shops like Rough Trade's old Portobello shack belting out dub and fanzines, late-night Soho gay Hi-NRG spinners Groove Records, Rock On with its collector's items for Kentish Town quiffabillies, Desmond's Hip City in Atlantic Road, Brixton, with its blue *'Blue Beat'* sign, and Lewisham's Dub Vendor, home of the great wordsmith, Smiley Culture, are social and cultural centres. And there is no sharp distinction between musicians whose lyrics have the force of poetry, like Elvis Costello, Billy Bragg and Marianne Faithfull (our generation's Sinatra), the poets who perform with music, like Linton Kwesi Johnson and Patti Smith, and poets who project their written work with the rhythmic fury and musical intensity of Benjamin Zephaniah and John Cooper Clarke. The subversive mix which surfaced first in punk and RAR went on from there into the (new) variety acts, political cabarets, poetry and oppositional comedy, and changed attitudes to language itself.

The post-war migration is the foreign body around which a new British identity is crystallising, quite beautiful to watch in its intricate, surprising sharp-edged flakes, shapes and angles. It arises from a series of negations. It was the artistic bankruptcy of the European-imitating petite bourgeoisie after independence that allowed Jamaica's national music to take such uncompromisingly rebel tones, remain resistant to dilution and then to reduplicate a distinctively UK idiom. It is the fact that black poetry and music was never deemed art which denied it formal preservation but which stamped it with an improvised and therefore experimental character. It is the theme of Empire-in-reverse which makes J. G. Farrell (who once observed, 'The loss of the British Empire is the only interesting thing that happened in my adult life') such an

Tosh.

See no evil.

Speak no evil.

Think no evil.

intriguing novelist, shapes so much post-war fiction in English from Lessing to Ballard and Rushdie and underlines our film makers' identification with the various chroniclers of the Raj.

In Britain there is not a single cultural riddle which can be solved without reference to imperial history. Because the human inheritors of that process are now part of what makes us us. The majestic sound-system operator Jah Shaka went to the quintessentially English Samuel Pepys School in South London, but his musical nom-de-sound comes from the warrior who reconstructed the Zulu armies in 1880. *No Problem*, the funniest British sitcom on TV, was written by an ex-Poona public schoolboy and a playwright born in Guyana and acted by the Black Theatre Co-operative. Innovation in modern London publishing has been shaped, from *OZ* through Pluto to Virago, by returned *colonials*, especially the Irish, who have brought with them spirit enough to radicalise even this most bourgeois of occupations. Bob Marley whirling biblical prophecies against Babylon in the Lyceum was only repatriating what the missionaries took out. And in the international sporting world one distinctive face of modern Britain is black, that of the athlete Daley Thompson, whose mixture of physical grace and witty disrespect inverts the traditional 'Anglo-Saxon' values.

And, although it is easiest to perceive there, it is not just a cultural question. Migration does not only replay and subvert the imperial era of British expansion but brings with it other echoes from our ever present past. If industrialists complain that the country is swamped with cheap manufactured goods, they ought to recognise that this is exactly what Britain did to Ireland in the nineteenth century. If the government bemoans the *flood of heroin*, they might understand that their predecessors fought wars to establish the right to supply the means of opium addiction in China. Port Stanley, *recaptured* in 1982, is part of the same historical process as Broadwater Farm, North London, *rioting* in 1985.

For it is surely impossible to comprehend the black-led uprisings in the inner cities without consideration of the emigration, annexation and conquest which created the empire, bankrolled metropolitan manufacture and bagged all those indefensible outpost islands. The upheaval which landed the O'Shaughnessys in the polo clubs of Buenos Aires and the McDonalds on the verandas of Poona brought the St Roses to play reggae in Bristol and the Begums to worship in Brick Lane.

But racism remains, more or less discreetly, an integral part of the make-up of the political and economic establishment in Britain. Indeed the eighties have been christened with a liberal sprinkling of Union Jackism as a distraction from and consolation for the new depression. The post-Scarman police are more assertive in their policing, the prisons pile higher, the Fleet Street press is still more abusive and black Britons remain excluded from whole areas of jobs and social life. Within weeks of office, Mrs Thatcher was brisk deporting wives and widows. Police chiefs talk about '**the coons**' and ministers describe Africa as '**bongo-bongo land**'. Surface adjustments, like say folding classes in primary schools and black kids in Smarties adverts, only go well, skin deep.

So, ironically, the first successes of the anti-racist movement in modern Britain have produced not our goal of greater harmony but a sharp polarisation. Nothing fundamental has changed, except for the worse. On one side is an increasingly bellicose and jingoistic white Anglo-Saxon Establishment with their horrific definitions of what being British means. On the other the modern dispossessed in communities which are being mortgaged to pay

Fed up down the Roman.

'And while the cruelties of the white man towards the black man are among the heaviest counts in the indictment against humanity, colour prejudice is not our original fault, but only one aspect of the atrophy of the imagination that prevents us from seeing ourselves in every creature that breathes under the sun.'
Doris Lessing

or Victorian ambitions ludicrously projected into the nuclear age. And this polarisation process, for which race is a touchstone, goes far beyond racial or even cultural issues and becomes more bitter and intractable as the depression rules out the possibility of old compromises.

There is a fight going on for the soul of our country. Those who uphold the *Old Britain*, that old gang, mortgage us to the irrelevant and dangerous symbolism of an imperial past. To keep up the payments they are quite prepared to dismantle the homes and schools and hospitals and industries which have shaped our past and made possible a useful future. Their rhetoric is of

Renewal, Resolution and Freedom, but the reality is millions of lives and human potentials reduced to scrabbling for survival as more and more tribute is rendered up to the armourers and the state. The National Health Service, comprehensive education, public support for the arts and so many other postwar reforms turn out to have been temporary, loaned to us on condition of good behaviour and now to be returned. Public endeavours are put back on the market place, collective values of tolerance and decency sold off in job lots, private greed raised to a national virtue even as the emotional tawdriness of the age of affluence becomes apparent.

And all this to preserve a culture which is truly alien; the shoddy, sham-rural of Home Counties Conservatism, the wonderful world of Harrods headscarves, muddy jodhpurs and the Ordinary Share Index, the Knightsbridge junkie, the casino lush and the bigot at the golf-club bar, Brylcreem and Montague Burton's bank-clerk suiting, the Soaraway *Sun* and the Sloane Rangers and *Stars on Sunday* and the eternal verities of the Queen Mum and the Mini Metro and Whitelaw and Whitehouse and Long May She Reign Over Us.

And in order to achieve this wonderful world, we are asked to accept as permanent the violent polarisation of wealth and power between a tiny minority of the 187 states in the world and the rest. And accept as inevitable the division within each nation between a tiny ruling minority and the mass of those who live and labour. As national solutions are shown to be impossible, we are fed more patriotism. As the world aches with shortage, we force feed our abdomens. As the globe longs for peace, we are prepared for war.

In the UK, *racism* is the issue which most keenly reflects these alternatives, the code which breaks this crisis in national personality. For racists, patriots and xenophobes, it allows a thought process which displaces the consequences of empire and conquest onto a visible minority who, along with 'the problem' itself, can be, literally, sent back into the historical limbo and abysmal ignorance from which, it is assumed, they impudently came to plague us. The Jew was made a symbol for usury. Black is a metaphor for everything that the white society cannot face in itself, its past, its passivity, its savagery and the strange emptiness of its murderous civilisation. Send them back. Because we can't face what they, silently, ask us about ourselves.

We whites must realise, before it is too late, that the reverse is true. That they are here because *we* were there. That there is no Britain without blacks and that we could not keep our slaves out of our sight for ever. That there is no such thing as pure English nationality or pure Scots or Welsh but a mongrel mix of invaders and predators and settlers and émigrés and exiles and migrants. That there is no *us* without *them*.

If our generation in the so-called United Kingdom is unable or unwilling to come to terms with our own history and not just endure or tolerate but embrace our fellow Britons from wherever with sincerity and delight, then we have no hope whatsoever of bringing about the larger changes we and the rest of the uncivilised world must make to survive and regenerate.

An alternative to racism will not be effective if it is presented by socialist who change sides, trade-union leaders who adopt the mentality of middle management, male revolutionaries who treat women like skivvies, or Marxist who turn socialism into something as obscure as particle mechanics. But without an alternative, the racist nightmare may become the waking truth as John Bull staggers into a vicious and absurd dementia, tripping over his wheezy bulldog, puking down his butcher's apron, trying to get hard fiddling with his nuclear fly buttons, gnashing his preposterous private-enterprise teeth in a bitter, self-parodying and painful rage unto death.

'The marvellous is everywhere, hidden from the eyes of the vulgar, but ready to explode like a time bomb.'
Benjamin Peret

Roy Peters

Cyril Regis, West Brom, and Billy Bonds, West Ham.

'Thus the awakening of the
dead in those revolutions
served the purpose of
glorifying the new struggles,
not of parodying the old; of
magnifying the given task in
imagination, not of fleeing
from its solution in reality: of
finding once more the spirit of
revolution, not of making its
ghost walk about once again.'
Karl Marx

T I M E   C H E C K

Abolition of slavery, **1772**

First Pan African Congress, London, **1900**
British Brothers League founded, Stepney, **1901**

Battle of Cable Street, **October 1933**

Commonwealth Immigrants Act, **1962**
National Front formed, **1967**
Enoch Powell's 'River of Blood' speech, **April 1968**
The May Events, Paris, **1968**

Bangladesh War of Independence, **1971**
Rock Against Racism founded, **August 1976**
'Anarchy in the UK' tour, **December 1976**
Battle of Wood Green, London, **April 1977**
Sex Pistols' 'Anarchy In The UK' at No. 1 in Jubilee week,
June 1977
Battle of Lewisham, **13th August 1977**
Anti Nazi League formed, **November 1977**
Victoria Park Carnival, London, **30th April 1978**
Brick Lane Solidarity Strike Against Racial Attacks, London,
July 1978
Brockwell Park Carnival, **24th September 1978**
Southall riot, Blair Peach killed, 342 charged, 700 arrested,
London, **23rd April 1979**
Thatcher elected, **24th April 1979**

St Paul's riot, Bristol, **April 1980**
Toxteth riots, Liverpool, **July 1981**
Battle of Orgreave, South Yorkshire, **28th May 1984**
Live Aid, **July 1985**
Handsworth riots, Birmingham, **September 1985**
Broadwater Farm riot, London, **October 1985**

HEROES AND VILLAINS

'**Art is not** a submission. It is a conquest.'
André Malraux

'**If you listen** to the blowing of
a Johny Hodges or the wailing of a
Bessie Smith you go right back to the old
negro spirituals and
right up to what Antony Braxton
and Cecil Taylor play today.'
Max Roach

N   A   M   E   C   H   E   C

With whom it was not impossible.
Bill Ash ■   Anthony Barnett ■ John Berger ▶
Andrew Bethell ■ The British Library ■   Elana Dallas ▶
Jan Dalley ■ Andy Dark ■   Ingrid von Essen
Denise Fenn ■ Michael Fenn ■ Bill Fishman ■
Mike Flood Page ■   Laurie Flynn ■ Nigel Fountain ▶
Gerry Gable ■ Ruth Gregory ■   Simon Guttman ▶
       Alistair Hatchett ■ Paul Holborow ■ Roger Huddle
Bob Humm ■ Dan Jones ■ Brenda Kelly ■ Bob Light ■
Melanie McFadyean ■ Jim Nichol ■   Joanna Rollo
    Black Rose ■   Mike Rosen ■ Raphael Samu
■ Nina Saunders ■   Red Saunders ■ Chris Schwartz
Searchlight ■ Syd Shelton ■   Siva Sivanandan
Socialist Worker ■   John Sturrock
          Paul Trevor ■ The Typing Pool ■
Kate Webb ■   Lucy Whitman